William Muirhead

China and the Gospel

William Muirhead

China and the Gospel

ISBN/EAN: 9783337166649

Printed in Europe, USA, Canada, Australia, Japan

Cover: Foto ©ninafisch / pixelio.de

More available books at **www.hansebooks.com**

CHINA AND THE GOSPEL.

CHINA

AND

THE GOSPEL.

BY THE

Rev. WILLIAM MUIRHEAD, M. Ed. Un. G. C.,

LONDON MISSIONARY SOCIETY.

LONDON:
JAMES NISBET AND CO., 21 BERNERS STREET.
1870.

CONTENTS.

CHAPTER I.
PRELIMINARY CONSIDERATIONS.

Object of the book—China—Name—Extent—Physical aspect—Climate—Antiquity—Population—Unity—Civilization—Government—Wealth and Resources—Place in history—Heathenism—Christian Missions 1

CHAPTER II.
LANGUAGE AND LITERATURE.

General characteristics—Mode of acquisition—Different sounds—Various dialects—Comparative antiquity—Time required for learning—Classic books—Other writings—Characters classified—Romanizing system—Spoken and written forms—English teaching—Diffusion of Chinese literature—Influence on native mind 28

CHAPTER III.
NATIONAL CHARACTER AND LIFE.

General aspect—Provincial differences—Prevailing torpor and immobility—Causes of it—Natural capacity—Moral standing and condition—Pride and prejudice—Aversion to change—Hostile bearing—Foreign policy—Missionary action ... 55

CHAPTER IV.
RELIGIOUS OPINIONS.

Treatment of the subject—Ideas of God—Creation—Providence—Moral government—Spiritual beings—Human Nature and Sin—Various forms of worship—Immortality and a Future state—Summary and results 79

CHAPTER V.
THE OPIUM TRAFFIC.

Its origin—Native and foreign opium—Physical, social, and moral effects—Religious bearing—Conduct of Chinese government—Legalization of the trade—Hindrance to Missionary work—Duty of Christian merchants 110

CHAPTER VI.
MISSIONARY WORK.

History of Missions to China—General opening of the country—Treaty rights—Translation and circulation of the Scriptures—Science and literature—Preaching—Itinerancies—Successes—Medical Missions—Schools—Female agency—Printing establishments 128

CHAPTER VII.
PERSONAL INCIDENT AND ADVENTURE.

First arrival—Study—Occurrences at Tsing-pu and Suchow—Pirates—Travelling—Yellow River—North China—Mongolia—Living Buddha—Jews—Conversions—Duke Kung—Chinese Scholar — Mahommedans — Strange questions — Mandarin peculation—Buddhist priests—Mathematician—Japan ... 161

CHAPTER VIII.
OBJECTIONS AND ANSWERS.

China not prepared for the Gospel—Denominationalism—Missionaries incompetent and idle—Wanting in self-denial—Married life—Missions expensive—Character of converts—The educational theory—Missionaries enthusiasts or rogues—Eternal punishment 199

CHAPTER IX.
REQUIREMENTS AND APPEALS.

China for Christ—Authority and encouragement—Wants of the Missionary cause—More time—More men and means—More union and co-operation in the field—More sympathy and intercourse at home—More earnest prayer and supplication ... 222

CHAPTER X.

MISSIONARY DISCOURSE.

"Where is the wise? where is the scribe? where is the disputer of this world? hath not God made foolish the wisdom of this world? For after that in the wisdom of God, the world by wisdom knew not God, it pleased God by the foolishness of preaching to save them that believe."—1 Cor. i, 20, 21 ... 255

APPENDIX.

The Divine Name—Chronology of China—Analogy of language—Character and influence of Confucius—The political state and prospects of China—The Christianisation of China 291

List of Protestant Missions in China 305

CHINA AND THE GOSPEL.

CHAPTER I.

PRELIMINARY CONSIDERATIONS.

Why publish a new book on this subject? The greatness of the theme, and our long practical acquaintance with it, form our only apology. We do not intend to discuss any of the profound and difficult points connected with the history, language, or philosophy of China; or expect to shed any considerable light on the peculiarities and social life of the people. Our aim precludes any anticipations of this kind. We have signified our object in the conjunction of China and the Gospel. We are desirous of bringing the two together. We are aware, to some extent, of the moral and spiritual necessities of the one, and the adaptation and sufficiency of the other to meet its case. This is our single idea. We recognize the bearing of it in the Missionary enterprise; and the unfolding of its difficulties, the rehearsal of its encouragements, the answers to various objections, with the exhibition of what it requires, and of the glorious prospects it holds out to view—all in reference to China—constitute the work we have proposed to ourselves in the following pages.

There are certain preliminary considerations necessary in order to apprehend the field of labour. There are particulars to be noticed about it, which do not equally apply to any other part of the world. We refer to the country of China, to the antiquity of its people, their number, unity, civilization, government, wealth, and resources, and their place in universal history, which may well enter into our estimate of the claims and obligations of the Missionary enterprise in relation to China.

The name given to the country by foreigners is not now applied to it by the natives themselves. They call it *Chung Kwoh*, or the Middle Kingdom; but the term in use by us corresponds to the designation given to it by various Asiatic nations from very early times. It answers to the name of the Tsin dynasty, whose chief is celebrated in history for having destroyed the feudal divisions of the country, and united them under his imperial sway about 250 B.C. His ancestry can be traced back as far as 642 years prior to that time, when the founder of it was invested with the sovereignty of the city of Tsinchau, in the north-west of China, and though his descendants greatly increased in power they continued to retain the same title. From the position and name of that city, as well as the dignity of the ruling power, it is likely that the whole country became known by the same appellation. There is every reason for believing that China was intended by the prophet Isaiah when he spoke of the "Land of Sinim."

China proper is situated on the eastern confines of Asia, and extends nominally from 18° to 40° north latitude, and from 98° to 124° east longitude. It comprehends an area of at least 1,800,000 square miles, or nearly 2,000,000 according to native calculation; but even this latter amount is not much more than two-fifths of the whole extent of the empire. It has under its dominion a number of countries with which we are very little, if at all, acquainted, and the entire area of the empire is estimated at no less than 5,300,000 square miles. China proper is divided into eighteen provinces, each of which is on an average as large as Great Britain. Its physical aspect is on a scale corresponding to the great size of the country. There are vast plains, towering mountains, magnificent rivers, beautiful streams, and immense lakes in different directions. In the outlying dependencies of Mongolia, Turkestan, Thibet, and Manchuria, there are some of the highest plateaux in the world, with far-reaching barren deserts and grassy lands, extending over thousands of miles. Though the soil varies much in different places, China is altogether one of the richest countries on the face of the earth. This may be owing in part to the industry of the inhabitants, but doubtless

4 PRELIMINARY CONSIDERATIONS.

the natural character of the soil is a primary occasion of it, and both seem necessary in order to meet the wants of the multitudes depending upon it for subsistence.

The climate of the country is a matter of much interest. The varieties of temperature are of course great, from the extreme south to the far distant north. In the former the hot weather lasts for a number of months, at times to an intense degree, while in the central and northern portions of the empire there are only two months of a really hot season, namely, July and August; the remainder of the year is pleasant and agreeable. During the winter, in the latter parts, the air is dry and bracing, and the residents readily gain strength again after the relaxing time of summer. The general salubrity of China is unquestioned by those who have had long experience of it, always allowing of course for the effects of change and other circumstances connected with a new and untried climate.

When China was first rendered accessible to foreigners, hopes were entertained by some that its antiquity would be found opposed to the established chronology of Western lands. The dates of Scripture were to be falsified, and a new era was in consequence heralded by them as about to dawn. It is true that the Chinese traditions spoke of thousands of years, during which various kings and emperors lived and reigned. As their history was examined, however, it appeared that there was no ground for these ancient pretensions. Their best writers did not admit them, and commenced their records only within moderate limits, all beyond was regarded as vague and fabulous. Though they could not trace their origin as a nation, their establishment in the country appears to have been at a time perfectly consistent with the older and more accredited chronology of the Bible. Of late years the subject has been carefully considered, by the study of the classic writings of China, and all the lights that can be brought to bear upon them; and it has been shown that the antiquity of the Chinese cannot be sustained beyond 2000 years before Christ. At that time they existed as a small community, in the north-west regions, living in a most primitive manner, yet even then the details are so few and uncertain that we cannot definitely speak of them until about 400 years after.

The earliest accounts contain narratives of the first two emperors, Yaou and Shun, who in their names and doings are looked upon by some as very doubtful existences. They may have been placed at the head of the record to give form and order to the history, and to serve as examples of all that was praiseworthy in public and in private life. They have certainly attained this honour in the estimation of the Chinese, and are always referred to as models of propriety in subsequent times. The Great Yu, who was probably the first real emperor of China, devoted himself to clearing the country of an overwhelming flood, which was likely an outbreak of the Yellow River, an event which has frequently happened, and on account of which it has been called "China's Sorrow." Having finished this work he entered diligently on other arrangements, tending to the regulation and prosperity of the empire; yet things are said to have been accomplished by him, in the course of his reign, that were only a tithe of them really effected, he must have been a man of extraordinary powers. We allude to these simply as showing the uncertainty of the early history of China, without denying the fact of its existence at the period in question. From the beginning of the Shang dynasty, nominally seventeen centuries before Christ, we have more reliable data to go upon, as the country was then assuming a settled and definite form, and much importance was attached to the records and archives of the nation.

The population of China is everywhere recognised to be immense. Four hundred millions are spoken of as the amount in round numbers, but an excess of even these figures is maintained by some as the actual calculation. There are registration boards hung up in every house, subject to the inspection of officers appointed for the purpose, whose work it is to make up the total aggregate from time to time, and send a report to head quarters. In view of the intelligence of the men engaged in it, and the nature of the methods employed to secure the most accurate returns, we are inclined fully to believe the estimate that is given in the general statistics. Every part of the country is under control. A complete system of government is established, from the Emperor down to the street and village constable, or tything man, who has the charge of ten houses; and great attention is paid to the enumeration of the people. As one travels through the towns, cities, and provinces of the country, he is convinced of the numerical greatness of the inhabitants. The social life in operation also is of a kind suited to the rapid increase of the population. Marriage is looked upon as highly proper in all cases, for the perpetuating of the family name, and the performance of ancestral sacrifice. The interests of the living and of the dead are alike consulted in the matter, and polygamy is allowed and practised within bounds, for the sake of the same object. Infanticide doubtless exists, but though we have no means of determining its amount, we do not think it materially affects the point in hand. Altogether we see no reason for denying the alleged populousness of China, and if we consider the size of the empire, and the provision made for the support of the people, there is nothing incongruous in the numbers that we have stated.

A further consideration is the unity and homogeneousness of the Chinese. This is a manifest characteristic, and appears in various ways. The Chinese were one people at the first, and they have maintained the same aspect to the present time. Their language and literature, their physiognomy and appearance, their civilization and culture, their intellectual, moral, and social affinities, all show an identity between them, both in kind and degree. The local differences existing among them in no wise militate against their essential national oneness. We see it at work in their high estimate of themselves, and in their strong antipathy to the rest of mankind. They are thoroughly of the same temper and disposition, trained and disciplined in the same manner, surrounded by and subject to the same influences, and retentive of the same peculiarities wherever they go. There is little or nothing of individuality about them. They form, as it were, a huge mountain mass, having the same general characteristics throughout, and not distinguished by the manifold varieties that obtain in other lands. At the same time it is not difficult to trace their ancient relationship to the nations or communities round about. There are resemblances to be seen betwixt the two, and in this way indeed to all the human family. The more the subject is investigated, the fact is made the more apparent, that "the whole world is kin,"—that "God hath made of one blood all nations of men, to dwell upon all the face of the earth," or as the Chinese say, "all within the compass of the four seas are brethren." Their language, customs and manners, moral and religious impressions, show this in a high degree, and there is nothing more peculiar in them than is to be accounted for by the state of isolation in which they have lived, and the circumstances connected with it for thousands of years.

Their civilization is described by themselves under the following four heads—*sze, nung, kung, shang*. The first denotes literature or the literary class, which is placed at the top of the list to indicate its extreme importance. It gives spirit and form, cast and character to the civilization of China. It applies to those who have devoted themselves to the study of the native classics, and includes all such, whatever be their rank or degree. They are of varied standing among themselves, but as a class exercise a dominant influence in the country, and command the respect and honour of all around them. They are trained, for the most part, in the primary schools, which are everywhere established, and besides there are public examinations held annually, or triennially, in the districts or departmental cities, to which thousands of students repair, in search of literary distinction. Only a moiety of the whole, about ten per cent. can possibly succeed, and the unsuccessful candidates often repeat the attempt till late in life. Many who have passed the first, or B.A. degree, which is called *Siu-tsai*, that is, blooming talent, will try to gain the M.A. standard, that is, *Keu-jin*, the elevated man, or a Licentiate. The further they go, the more searching and severe is the examination required, and comparatively few reach the still loftier positions, such as the *Tsin-sze*, or the doctorate, and the *Han-lin*, or forest of pencils, which is equivalent to membership in the Imperial Academy, and has nothing corresponding to it among ourselves. As advance is made, however, in these literary examinations, there is an increased value attached to it, and the student becomes eligible for higher official appointments and Imperial favour. Limited though the range of study appears to be from our point of view, it demands the intensest application, and leaves its mark on the character and standing of the men engaged in it.

The second in order is agriculture or the farming class. It occupies this position from its importance in raising the necessaries of life. Much encouragement is given to it, and at stated times the emperor in the capital, and his mandarins throughout the empire, set an example to the farmers at large, by handling the plough and sowing the seed in some adjacent field. Whatever may be said as to the peculiarity and unchangeableness of their farming operations, or as to their admitting of much improvement in the implements and methods employed, the fact is that this class deserves high commendation for their diligence and success. Their cultivation of the various cereals for native use, and of the valuable commodities for which the outside world is so largely indebted to them, speaks volumes in their favour; and there are many things in which an interchange of thought with them might be of service to their compeers among ourselves.

The third is the artistic or handicraft population. Their part is to manufacture as that of the last was to produce, and looking at the requirements and attainments of such a great nation as the Chinese, in their houses, canals, bridges, weaving, embroidery, and other things, we are not disposed to under-rate this class, in respect of the comforts and conveniences of social life. Of course there are not the same ideas prevalent in China, as to household arrangements and works of public utility, that obtain in our own country. As it is, however, we observe the Chinese in this department skilful and ingenious in a high degree. They are capable also of acquiring our ideas in almost all branches of artistic and mechanical labour, and are largely employed in this way in our various foreign settlements.

The mercantile class is placed next, from its being considered of lower standing than those already mentioned. Its object is simply to negotiate the productions and manufactures of the previous two classes, but its operations are of great value and importance. So far as the appearance in the villages, towns, and cities is concerned, it might reasonably strike one that the Chinese was a nation of shopkeepers. They are given to trading in all manner of things, on a large and on a limited scale. It would seem as if their disposition in this line were naturally ingrained in them; and they carry it into the countries round about, where they are the financiers and merchants of the community. Our own connection with them in this respect is very extensive. Their tradal interests at the different treaty ports amount to many millions sterling a year, and admit of being indefinitely increased. They are found to be shrewd and calculating in their habits, and fully equal to play their part in the matter. Though much may not be said of their honesty and truthfulness, when selfish considerations intervene, yet the fact of their being able to meet the foreigner on his own ground, and transact such an enormous business with him as they do, shows their wonderful capacity and power. It is with this class that our merchants come specially into contact, and they are beginning to influence it in the adoption of various elements of our western civilization. The Chinese merchants largely avail of our foreign steamers and sailing vessels, and were it possible to command the assent of the imperial authorities, there is no doubt that they would enter readily into the construction of railways and telegraphs, which with other things would be of mighty service in breaking down the exclusiveness of the native manners, and introducing a new era in the social life of China.

The civilization thus referred to is of varied antiquity. Among the first individuals mentioned in history we find celebrated names, such as Fu-he, Shin-nung, and Hwang-te, who, though very doubtful personages, are spoken of as the authors of several useful arts. They are in consequence highly honoured, and worshipped according to the state ritual in temples erected for the purpose in different places. It is well known, though not to be wondered at, that the Chinese were the first discoverers or inventors of printing, gunpowder, and the mariners' compass. They have not made that full use of them, it is true, which we have been led to do; still they form important elements in their civilization, and taking them altogether, the Chinese stand far ahead of every other people separated from the moulding and stimulating influences of our Divine Christianity.

What is the government of China? The answer is that it is imperial. The emperor is at the head of affairs, and the succession is dependent on his appointment, which is not always in the natural line, or in the order of sonship. He is regarded as the father of his people, and so the government is called patriarchal. This, indeed, is the basis and characteristic of all law and order in China, alike in the house and the state. In the administration, and connected with the court, there is an inner or privy council, and a general cabinet, under which there are six boards established in the capital, whose departments are respectively—civil offices, revenue, war, punishments, rites and ceremonies, and public works. At present the emperor is a minor of sixteen years of age, and the empress dowager, with the real mother of the emperor, form a regency. They are said to be very able in the management of affairs. The office of censorship is an important element in the government. Those connected with it are at liberty freely to address the emperor, and to state their views as to the general condition of things. This exercises a controlling and beneficial influence in the public councils, and over the conduct of the ruling mind. It cannot be rashly interfered with even by the emperor, though in consequence of its being unwisely administered, he has the power of depriving the individuals of their official rank. The eighteen provinces of China proper are divided into eleven governments, over which there are eight governors-general, and fifteen lieutenant-governors, while there is a complete gradation of civil and military officers in connection with them. The same system obtains more or less in the outlying territories. There is nothing loose or uncertain, so far as the machinery of state is concerned. Each element of it has its appropriate place. Each member of the constitution has his distinct and special office. The laws in operation, too, are well defined, or arrangements are made whereby the rule of equity may be observed, as fairly and wisely as possible. Much liberty is granted to the various officials in the discharge of their duties, but it is urged that the interests of the people be carefully and honestly considered, as well as the honour and integrity of the government maintained.

Though the constitution of empire may be well and wisely formed, the course of it is far from being well and wisely carried on. The great number of officials are chargeable with peculation, extortion, and the prosecution of their own selfish ends and objects. They show little concern for the real welfare of those over whom they are placed, and are, first of all, mindful of the profits they can make in connection with their office. They are allowed very little emolument, and having large expenses to meet, from the numerous dependents hanging upon them, and from the bribes they are expected to pay their superiors, they adopt all possible measures to answer these ends, as well as to secure an ample competency for themselves when called to retire from the cares of public life. It is indeed a wonder often how government goes on at all with such a set of men as are thus connected with it. We can account for it only from the excellence of the system itself, and from the fact that there is much shrewdness, and tact, and ability shown in all departments, meeting one point and another as they come up, and employing every available expedient to avoid difficulties or remedy mistakes. The people have been accustomed to this line of things, and know no better, yet they often groan under it, and when they have a choice of two men they fail not to express their ideas of them in a very intelligible way.

The government is no doubt despotic and arbitrary on many occasions, but it does not in general ignore the views and necessities of the people. In the absence of anything like popular representation, the voice of the country comes to be heard, and it has been a fundamental maxim from the earliest times, that the sympathies of the people are to be taken as an index of the will of Heaven being on the side of the governing power. Many dynasties have been established or overthrown on this ground. The principle exerts a wholesome restraint upon the exercise of despotic power, and is an inducement to deal kindly and leniently towards those under its control. The great object of the government, however, is to repress outbreaks and maintain peace, which is often done in a manner that seems to us unreasonably harsh and severe. Were the ruling classes more honest and more moderate in their extortions, there would doubtless be less rebellion in the empire, and less occasion for the summary punishments that are inflicted on a wide-spread scale.

The wealth and resources of China is a matter of special importance, both from the home and foreign aspect of it. There are official documents from which information on the subject can be drawn, but they are necessarily incomplete and partial. We cannot rely on them as in the case of our own national statistics. It is sometimes said that about one half of the population have work enough to fight the battle of life. The struggle for mere existence on their part is hard, notwithstanding the apparent cheapness of their mode of living. As to the other half, the great majority are in comfortable circumstances, while there are many reputed to be enormously wealthy in land and other property. The means of making money in China are in the ordinary way of trade and commerce, agriculture and the like. There are numbers, too, in official life, who become rich from their peculation of public money, and other illegal acts. Judging from the aspect of things in large cities, and in the general condition of the country, one is satisfied that there is a vast amount of wealth in circulation. The industrial operations of the empire are great and manifold. There are ten thousand ways in which these are carried on, and as many articles in use forming the staple or material of the whole.

The land tax is the principal source of revenue to the government, and varies according to the productiveness of the soil. It was stated some years ago to be about £12,000,000, and is payable in coin or in grain, which is forwarded to Pekin as imperial tribute. Taxes are also imposed on the ordinary branches of trade to a degree that is often found extremely burdensome to the people. They are sometimes levied in an arbitrary and capricious manner, professedly to meet the current exigencies of the empire, but a large portion of the amount is known to be appropriated by the officials. The authorities will frequently "squeeze," as it is called, the rich men in the neighbourhood, to the extent of thousands of pounds sterling, and there is no redress or appeal. Foreign commerce is subjected to taxation over and above the legal imposts to a degree that almost paralyses it in the interior. The various mandarins lay a tax on the goods that pass through their particular jurisdiction, and the native merchant is thus severely fleeced, both in what he buys and in what he sells. The foreign customs yield the annual amount of three millions sterling to the imperial exchequer, and the current value of imports and exports under this head for the past year was equal to forty-five millions, but this may be regarded as only a moiety of the possible development of trade. The entire revenue of the Chinese government was stated by Sir G. Staunton at £66,000,000, of which about £12,000,000 were remitted to Pekin. In 1867, the whole amount was estimated at only £20,000,000.

Some inquiry has been made as to the mineral resources of the northern portion of the country, and it appears that there are at least 84,000 square miles of coals alone in that part, independently of many other valuable products. And this is no more than an indication of what obtains elsewhere in great abundance. Were the restrictions laid on the opening of mines and the formation of improved modes of transit withdrawn, there is no doubt that China would be found to be one of the richest countries in the world, for all kinds of mineral wealth; but until changes and improvements take place in the way pointed out by foreign science, the country must remain in its present fixed, stationary, and imperfectly developed state.

The bearing and influence of China on other nations, or its place in universal history, ought not to be passed over. It may seem as if little could be said on this subject, from the strange isolation of the country, but as the matter is studied we find that it is very otherwise. Looking to remote times and places, it appears that China did not consider itself, and was not regarded, as alone in the earth. There were embassies that came to it from imperial Rome, and endeavours were made by it to reciprocate them. Commerce was transacted with India, Ceylon, Arabia, and other countries at an early period. Central Asia was largely affected by some of its great military heroes. About 2,000 years ago, under the fifth emperor of the Han dynasty, the empire of China was much more extensive than it is now. It embraced the larger portion of inhabited Asia to the west of the Caspian Sea, inclusive of Siam, Pegu, Camboya, and Bengal. When the Mongols usurped the government in the twelfth century, they carried their arms and their influence far and wide in connection with it. In the mediæval ages, the attention of Western countries was drawn to it, and the foreign intercourse carried on since that time is well known to all.

But we wish to note the subject not from the casual or occasional extension of power and trade into other parts. We want to show the manifest bearing of China through the ages on surrounding countries. This sphere alone is large enough for our observation. Though the civilization of China has led it to exclude itself from the rest of the world, it appears that it has exerted a mighty influence on the language, manners and customs, moral and religious character of many other places. It is astonishing the similarity thus existing between the Chinese and the inhabitants of the ultra-Gangetic countries, Japan, Corea, and the numerous Tartar communities to the north and west of it. Such was its dignified position, such were its arrogant yet acknowledged claims, that it has been considered a duty and a privilege in the case of these nations from time immemorial to send tribute to China, and confess their great inferiority in comparison. Any inattention on their part has often been punished in a summary manner, while the military power of the Middle Kingdom has been extended with varied success among tribes and peoples, with whose names and localities we are little, if at all, acquainted. We are accustomed to determine the importance of any Western kingdom, by its place and history in relation to countries and events known to us, but China and its surroundings have been alike shut out from the sphere of our vision till comparatively a recent period; and we are not to undervalue the bearing and influence of a great country in the East, because of our ignorance of it in the West. As we become familiar with the facts of the case, we observe China all along a vast and populous empire on the borders of Eastern Asia, exerting a dominant sway in the neighbouring countries, whose laws and languages, habits and practices, are interwoven with elements thoroughly Chinese, and whose inhabitants have been accustomed to speak in the highest terms of the might and greatness of the Flowery Land. Whether these inhabitants originally were part and parcel of the Chinese nation, branches of the same common stock, separated members of the same family, or whether they were simply affected and influenced by the overwhelming shadow of its government and civilization, we shall not now seek to inquire. Only we find in the East the widely extended ramifications of Chinese power in a great variety of ways, and as we are accustomed to speak of the Assyrian, Greek, and Roman empires in former days, exerting their sway in all directions, so we have equal warrant to speak of the ancient and far-reaching Chinese empire, and of its thus occupying a most important place in the general history of the world. However we may disregard its culture and civilization, it is otherwise in the case of its own immense population, and of the numerous tribes and nations round about, whose character and attainments were judged of by their intercourse with, and their conformity to, the line of things observed in China. However we may boast of the history and influence of our own and other countries in the West, we are not at liberty to underrate the actual value of the history and influence of the great Chinese empire in its particular position. And there is a point not to be overlooked, namely, that in our own days, the products, the commerce, and even the politics and emigration of China, are exerting a growing power in the social life of England and America. China is being felt mightily in its relations to the most distant and most civilized nations on the face of the earth. Though these relations may be forced upon the people, it is by a law of Providence, and there is ample material in China for its wielding an influence in the West, such as it has done for ages in the East, corresponding to its own greatness and wealth and culture. Let us hope that it will be understood in its proper light, and that its place in the family of nations will be such as it is capable of occupying, under the modifying, enlightening, and renovating influences of Christendom.

This leads us to notice that the Chinese people, in connection with all these striking and peculiar characteristics, are essentially a heathen people— heathen in the fullest and saddest sense of the term. As we shall have occasion to show, they were originally possessed of the knowledge of God, and have the evidences of His Being and Perfections, His over-ruling Providence and Moral Government recorded in their ancient classics, and in the minds and consciences of the people; yet the great truth has been overgrown by succeeding and surrounding elements in their daily life and practice. They are literally in the condition of the Ephesians, prior to their conversion to Christianity, "without hope and without God in the world." They now know not God. They have lost the knowledge of Him and all the sublime impressions connected with it. They are either imbedded in atheism and materialism, or are given over to idolatry and superstition of many and various kinds. All their native literature and learning, all their wisdom and philosophy, of which they boast so much, and which have made them a highly civilized and enlightened people in some respects, have utterly failed to emancipate them from the thraldom of these moral and spiritual evils, or to prevent their subjugation by them entirely. We are convinced with the Apostle in regard to the religious state of ancient Greece and Rome, that it has been the same with the Chinese. Their very wisdom and philosophy, their speculations and vain imaginings, have been the direct occasion of bringing them into their present state of ignorance and error, as to the only true and living God.

If such be the case with them in the matters of natural religion, they are still more wretched and wanting in a Christian point of view. In this respect, "darkness covers the earth, and gross darkness the people." They have no right conception of the evil of their state, and they have no idea of the only availing antidote to it. Ages have passed away in their history, during which all the resources of the native mind have been tried and taxed to the utmost, all the learning and influences of a peculiar and high-toned civilization have been employed to remedy the misery of China, but it can be said with truth, they have been employed in vain. China is not only no better, it is actually worse. The evil is augmenting. Its condition is more deplorable than ever it was. The systems long in operation for its moral and religious improvement are now growingly effete. They have had their day. Their vital and energizing power appears to have ceased, if ever it really existed, and there is nothing to be seen all over the land, but the wide-spread indications of spiritual death. We are everywhere as in the valley of vision, which was "full of dry bones, and lo! they were very dry."

This suggests to us the motives and considerations of the missionary enterprise—the duties and obligations connected with it. There is the sad, the doleful condition of four hundred millions of our fellow men just referred to, and which we shall have occasion more fully to delineate. It is their highest good that is contemplated by the work in question—their intellectual, moral, spiritual, and eternal well-being. This is embraced by the Missionary enterprise in a sense that no other scheme of human organization has in view. Whatever else may be proposed or carried out for the enlightenment of the nation and the development of the country, we hail as contributing to the specific end of the Christian Missionary. We gratefully acknowledge all the political, mercantile, scientific, and mechanical influences brought to bear on China, and which tend in any way to raise it in the scale, and ameliorate the wretchedness and misery, or dispel the ignorance and error, that universally prevail. These we regard as subservient, in the course of Divine Providence, to the grand object that is now before us. The whole has this one ultimate bearing and application, and however apparently disconnected with or opposed to it, we believe that they will be over-ruled for the accomplishment of this mighty and magnificent result.

It is, however, a matter of first importance in our view, that the Missionary work has specially to do with the conversion of men to God, their spiritual recovery and restoration, their reclamation from the evils and errors of heathenism and idolatry, the regeneration of their hearts and lives, the renewed devotement of their powers and faculties to the service of their Maker, and the preparation of their whole being for the blessedness of heaven. All this we are persuaded can be effected only by Divine agency, through the preaching and reception of the everlasting Gospel. This is the appointed instrumentality, and it is the object of the Missionary enterprise chiefly to employ this means, and herald the tidings of salvation through a crucified Redeemer to the ends of the earth. Whatever men may say about it, however they may deride its necessity or its suitability, call it if they will "the foolishness of preaching," we are satisfied as to its being a Divine command, strengthened and intensified in its authority and obligation by the circumstances in which it was given, and the Person, character, and work of Him who imposed it on His followers. We recognise His supreme and absolute right in the matter. We bow in lowly allegiance to Him in regard to it. We consider it our highest honour and privilege, as well as our greatest duty, to obey His gracious mandate, while we lament our very feeble and imperfect compliance with it. We acknowledge in the Missionary enterprise a divine commission full of grace and mercy to the human race. Mysteries indeed attend it at every step. We are at a loss to account for many things connected with it, but this is no concern of ours. The marching orders are clear and imperative. The greatest interests are at stake in carrying them out. For all practical purposes, the promises of God, the travail of the Redeemer's soul, the truth of Christianity, and its extension in the earth, are involved in the carrying out of this great enterprise. It impels us to grand and noble deeds by the highest and holiest considerations. The parting command of our blessed Lord includes the whole. "All power is given unto me in heaven and on earth. Go ye, therefore, and disciple all nations, and lo! I am with you alway, even unto the end of the world."

CHAPTER II.

LANGUAGE AND LITERATURE.

In prosecuting the Missionary work in China, we have various and peculiar difficulties to contend against, and we proceed to the enumeration of the most important of these. We may classify them under the following heads, the language and literature of the country, the national character and life of the people, their religious ideas, and the opium traffic. We need not advert to the natural moral state and condition of the Chinese, as forming a barrier to the spread of the gospel. It exists everywhere, with perhaps equal intensity, and is experienced in connexion with all Christian effort, alike at home and abroad. Our object is to individualize our case, and show the peculiar difficulties in the way of the Missionary enterprise in China.

We refer to the language and literature of China, in the first place, as it stands at the very threshold of our work, and must be encountered at the outset of our labours.

We are not about to consider the Chinese language in its peculiar structure or component parts. This has been well shown in various books written for the purpose; only we may observe, that it is, in our view, the oldest of living languages, and the nearest akin to the original mother tongue. It is in a historic, as well as constituent sense, the language of infancy, monosyllabic in its character, and composed of roots and elements which have existed from the beginning, without any essential variation or change. This has been the case, notwithstanding its high antiquity and extensive use, by the most populous nation in the world. It has been studied, cultivated, and employed, to an extent perhaps beyond comparison, but it retains all its early characteristics, and no modification or change appears to have come over it in the lapse of ages. This may be accounted for, in part, by the long isolation of the people, though their own national differences might, as in other countries, have served to affect it, or the fixed and uniform civilization that has existed in the country may have given a corresponding aspect to the language; but after all, it appears that the occasion of it is to be found in the essential structure of the language itself. It has no alphabetic basis. It is the expression of things in the most natural and definite form, and it has maintained this principle, just as if a child had used it in early days, full allowance being made for the expansion of thought and feeling in after life. The written characters have undergone various changes, as they are more the result of artificial labour, and have thus been subject to many adventitious influences, brought to bear upon them. Speaking of the literary style as a whole, it has been stereotyped and fixed in its main features by the ancient classic writings, which have all along been studied by the scholars of China, and imitated in the fullest manner.

The spoken and written forms require to be learned, in order to render a Missionary effective in the prosecution of his work. The former, apparently simple and easy at first, is found to be very otherwise as progress is made. We never met a person who knew anything about it, except as the result of close and prolonged study. Other languages, such as the Japanese, the Malay, and the Hindustanee, can be acquired, to some extent, by means of ordinary intercourse; but it is not so with the Chinese. Whether this is owing to the monosyllabic form of the words, that cannot be laid hold of by a casual hearer, or to any other cause, we are at a loss to discover, only it does require a great amount of attention and study. A good memory, a good ear, in a linguistic sense, and a good voice, are indispensable to a good speaker of Chinese. The manner in which it is generally learned is the following.

A native teacher is engaged, who pronounces one, two, or more words at a time, the sound of which the foreign student endeavours to imitate. At first he may commit a number of mistakes, from not giving the right tonal accent or emphasis peculiar to the phrase, or perhaps any correct correspondence to the words at all. The teacher perseveres in the utterance of the sounds, and the scholar after repeated attempts, it may be, succeeds in a close imitation of the original. Thus the work goes on day by day, and month after month, for hours together, in the course of which an acquaintance is formed with a great variety of words, and the meanings attached to them. The colloquial medium, or the native dialect of the place in which the student is residing, and the mandarin or court dialect, are thus learned, by means of books published in these forms, or written by the teacher for the study of his particular pupil. At the beginning of one's study of the Chinese language, it is desirable that the colloquial medium, in one form of it or another, should be acquired, and it is recommended that it be done by means of the native character. This will facilitate the knowledge of it when the literature of the country is entered on, and enable the student more correctly to give the pronunciation, than by writing the sounds in English.

The native scholar acquires his reading powers in a similar manner. He is set from the first day of his student life to pronounce the Chinese character in the orthodox style. He follows the teacher a number of times, and submits to correction until it is no longer necessary; and so he goes over the extensive range of his native classics. The work proceeds in his case for many years, during which time he is never taught the meaning of the words he learns, or the books he is told to rehearse or memorize. That would be regarded at his age and with his attainments, as an impossible and useless task, to be performed in course of time. Our opinion is greatly in favour of this line of things, formed as the Chinese written language is, so differently from the spoken style. But the native scholar has no occasion to learn his mother tongue at school. It is not that department that is cultivated at all. Doubtless there is greater correctness and propriety in his mode of talking it, when he has acquired the elements of a polite education. There are, however, no books published in the native dialect, except it be of an obscene and vulgar kind, or a few in the mandarin form of the language, which is never taught in the schools. It is only the high classical style that is there read and studied. In the case of the foreign student it is very otherwise. He is desirous of learning the colloquial medium, the common language of the people, and he has to do it by dint of close and arduous application. The sound and sense of it are alike to be acquired, and at the same time. It is often proper for him to read for several hours consecutively, in imitation of the teacher, so as to get the exact sound and rhythm of the words, but he has to give a large portion of his time besides, to find out the meaning of what he reads, even though it be in the colloquial talk.

The different sounds of the Chinese spoken language vary from four hundred and eleven in the mandarin, to as many as eight hundred in the different vernaculars. These admit of being indefinitely increased, by means of the tonal accentuations, which enter so essentially into the structure of the language. Too much importance cannot be attached to this on the part of the student. Some acquire the precise tone of each word scientifically and thoroughly, others pick it up more from habit and practice in a general way, but in that case with varying correctness. There is no doubt that some of the dialects require the tonal accents to be pronounced more clearly and forcibly than others, but the accents obtain equally and essentially in the whole. In the different dialects the number and sound of the tones are very unlike. There are dialects in which four upper and four lower tones are to be found, they correspond to each other in a high and low division; while there are dialects in which four upper tones and only one lower tone exist. The real intonation of the words also often varies in connection, according to well determined rules. Besides the tones, that are an indispensable portion of the language, though called by the same names in every instance, differ widely in the actual sounds attached to them. An upper even tone, or an upper high tone, in one

D

part of the country, does not resemble the same tone in another part; and so the locality of an individual may be determined by his dialect in this as well as in other respects. These tones are necessary, in order to the multiplication of words, and the facility of communication, at the same time they are not the only guides to the apprehension of the meaning. The context is of great importance in the matter, and it often occurs that a person not conversant with the precise tones of his words will express himself far more clearly and satisfactorily than another who is systematically acquainted with the whole. He is in this case very much like the common people themselves, who though speaking correctly and intelligently, are not able to indicate the exact intonation of the words they speak. In both instances the habit is acquired by constant practice, and the foreign student is immensely aided in his endeavours to speak properly, by reading with his teacher, and mingling with the natives, so as to learn their precise mode of expression. Some of our best scholars acknowledge that their aptitude in speaking was formed chiefly in this way.

It may be proper to say something here in reference to the different dialects existing in the country. We start on the understanding that the language of China is emphatically one, in its monosyllabic and syntactical forms. The very words are the same in the great majority of instances, allowing for slight variations of a local kind; but the mode of pronouncing them often differs so much that persons coming from a few miles distance apart are occasionally at a loss in communicating with each other. In general, however, it is not so, only as one recedes from a place, the peculiarities of dialect increasingly appear. The acquisition of one greatly assists in the attainment of another, for the language is essentially the same, and it is required, for the most part, simply to vary the sound or tone of the word, or in the absence of another term the mannerism of the sentence, to enable the learner intelligibly to express his meaning. There is often great difficulty in shaking off the peculiar twang or brogue of one's original dialect. It clings tenaciously to the speaker, like a man's native tongue at home, and in all his after endeavours he may still be known as having belonged to another part of the country. There are not a few, however, of our best students who have overcome their anglicised style of speaking, and the peculiarities of any single dialect they may have previously learned, while they talk freely and fully in another. It is gratifying that so far as Missionary work is concerned, the colloquial medium of the place where the Missionaries are, suffices in the case of many millions of the people. The varieties to be met with in the immediate neighbourhood, or even at a considerable distance, are not always so great as to be an obstacle in the way of understanding them. At the same time parties often come to hear us from remote places, who can scarcely, if at all, apprehend our meaning in the *patois* of the district. It is desirable in these circumstances to learn another dialect, and the qualifications of the speaker are thus greatly increased. Mandarin is most useful in this way. It admits of being spoken, with slight variations, over many of the provinces, each comprising a population of about twenty millions, and the knowledge of it enables a Missionary both to communicate with persons from a distance, and to travel far and wide in the prosecution of his work.

An inquiry has been started as to the antiquity of the various dialects—which has the priority of date on its side? The question is perhaps of the same kind with the prevailing form of the English language, compared with any of the current *patois*. Our own opinion is in favour of the present mandarin or court dialect, being the most ancient, and on the following grounds. We find it spoken over by far the greater part of China, with various modifications, extending from the north-western provinces, which were first occupied by the Chinese, on their entrance into the country. It has received the greatest cultivation, and is most nearly allied to the book style. It admits of being more correctly printed in the native character than any other dialect, and its use from early times among the governing classes, is an argument in its favour. The more southern dialects have the same essential characteristics, but are in their sounds far more vulgar and uncouth than the bold and scholar-like mandarin of the north, or the plaintive and polite style of the central districts. These southern dialects contain indications also of early departure from the ruling tongue of the more civilized and cultivated regions; and have words and phrases connected with them which bear evidence of a local and later origin. Still, in either case, the date is very ancient, and all the dialects are offsprings of the same common stock, which have retained their peculiarities for many centuries.

As to the length of time that may be required to learn the language, it varies of course in different individuals. In about a year some make considerable progress, so that they can converse in a general way with their teachers, and are intelligible on a number of ordinary topics. It requires a much longer period, however, to be able to speak with freedom and fulness on the various subjects that come up. There are those who never attain the desired facility, and this may arise from a natural incapacity on their part, while there are others who in their particular spheres can converse and preach with the greatest fluency. It appeared to them at first as if it were well nigh impossible to frame their tongues, so as to give utterance to their ideas in a rhythmical and orderly style, like the Chinese, but they are a wonder to many from the interesting and intelligent manner in which they talk and preach. We have known foreigners who have been mistaken by the natives as belonging to themselves, from their accurate and ready command of the language; and it is gratifying that such a facility is more or less within the reach of all, in a Missionary point of view. Some may deny it from the meagre acquisitions of persons whom they have heard, or from their own shortcomings in the matter, yet the facts of the case remain as have been stated. The truth is that the Word of Life is being communicated in the language of China to myriads and millions of the people, by means of foreign Missionaries, in a style that they can readily understand, and in many instances warmly appreciate.

The literature of the country now comes before us for consideration. It requires to be attentively examined, in order to convey a right idea of its character and bearing on the work of Christian missions. As a whole it is of colossal size and enormous difficulty. The classic department lies at the bottom of all the culture and civilization of China. Its study is diligently prosecuted by the scholars or teachers of the country; it gives tone and bias to their modes of thought, and to all the other literature that has succeeded it in the lapse of ages. After the foreign Missionary has acquired a measure of acquaintance with the colloquial medium, it is a duty on his part to enter on the study of these classic books. There are a few elementary works, which are put into the hands of the Chinese youth, to familiarize them with a number of the native characters. These may or may not be gone into by the foreign missionary, but the classics are proposed to him with all gravity and solemnity by the Chinese teacher.

The first in order is the *Ta-yiŏh* or the Great Learning. It begins thus:—"What the Great Learning teaches is to illustrate illustrious virtue; to renovate the people, and rest in the highest excellence. The point where to rest being known, the object of pursuit is then determined; and that being determined, a calm imperturbedness may be attained. To that calmness there will succeed a tranquil repose. In that repose there may be careful deliberation, and that deliberation will be followed by the attainment of the desired end. Things have their root and their completion. Affairs have their end and their beginning. To know what is first and what is last will lead near to what is taught in the Great Learning." These ideas are illustrated in a variety of ways bearing on personal virtue, on through a course of world-wide influence, until the whole country is thereby brought into circumstances of peace and order. The second book is the *Chung-yung* or the Doctrine of the Mean, wherein the laws of harmony are detailed in the life and character, especially of the perfect man—the sage for example, with the teachings of his moral nature and the supreme will of Heaven. The *Lun-yu,* or the Confucian analects, recounts the sayings of the master with his disciples and others, in which his views and opinions on a number of subjects are brought forward. The books of Mencius contain the writings of one of China's greatest men. He is, however, only a philosopher, not a sage in the proper sense of the term. He is looked upon as subordinate, in moral and literary rank, to Confucius, whom he succeeded in time, and whose sentiments he adopted in the fullest manner. The above series forms in all four books, and following them are the five classics. The first of these is the *Shu-king,* or the Book of History, which narrates the chief events of Chinese History from the dawn of empire to 721 B.C. The second is the *She-king,* or the Book of Poetry, which also gives the earliest extant pieces of poetical writing contained in the language. The *Yih-king,* or the Book of Changes, professes to furnish an account of the changes that take place in physical nature, according to certain figures or diagrams, that were determined in ancient Chinese philosophy. The *Le-ke,* or the Record of Rites and Ceremonies, gives us information as to the ancient forms, to which Confucius was greatly attached, and which he inculcated upon his disciples. The *Chun-tsew,* or the Book of Spring and Autumn, is a history by Confucius of his native state Loo, from 722 to 484 B.C.

These various classic books reaching back in some instances to three or four thousand years ago, have been commented on in after days by most distinguished men, whose commentaries under imperial sanction are bound up with the original, and studied in common with it. They give tone and colour to the ancient text, and without them it would be of very doubtful interpretation in many parts. They are not universally accepted yet as they have received the royal *imprimateur* for about seven hundred years, and furnish the authorized standard explanation of the text, they are officially adhered to. A lamentable feature of these commentaries is the irreligious spirit pervading them. They are atheistic or materialistic in their character and tendency—an element that does not accord with the ideas of the more ancient classic books, but such are the views now everywhere prevailing in consequence, and we find in them a chief difficulty in the way of Christianity. We shall have occasion to allude to this subject again.

In addition to these classic writings and the commentaries attached to them, there is a vast amount of native literature, and in great variety. The student may proceed far in his researches into this field, and doubtless he will find much that is interesting, if not positively instructive. The whole range of Chinese literature is divided into the classics, histories, philosophies, and the *belles lettres*. Under each of these heads there is an indefinite series of works, extending over many thousands of volumes, and presenting in all a wonderful development of intellectual power. We would here call attention to Mr. Wylie's notes on Chinese literature, which go over the whole field in a very able and useful manner. We confess that his review fills us with astonishment. We see in these native writings, their style, their import, and their number, the ground on which the Chinese boast so highly of their literary attainments, and of their supposed superiority in this respect to all other nations. Foreign students cannot possibly enter at length into this extended range of Chinese literature, but if inclined to investigate any matter of philology, or philosophy, or history, as bearing upon the social life and manners of the people, they will find ample scope for the purpose. Of course the whole is thoroughly Chinese. Little or nothing is to be gained from it in the way of information regarding other countries, except it may be in the immediate neighbourhood, from which we have been shut out for ages. But the Chinese accounts of these countries must be taken with modification. Their literature is chiefly of a philosophic kind, intellectual and moral, rather than physical and observational. It has to do with men more than with things. Their natural science is crude and puerile. They have no tendency in that direction. It is not encouraged by the official *regime*. It is not in accordance with the ancient teachings. It is of no practical value to them in the business of life. The mind of China has been exercised for the most part upon itself, and not upon the works of nature, as a study, or as a pursuit, or as an object of knowledge.

We consider it important that a Missionary should inform himself as to certain portions of the lighter literature which is everywhere read, and goes far to make the Chinese character what it is. We are inclined to attach great value in this point of view to various historical romances, novels, and such like books, which, in a simple, easy style, betray many of the worst elements of human nature, and being read with the greatest avidity by all classes, tend to demoralize the people to a fearful extent. We have been often asked how it is that the Chinese are so untruthful, dishonest, mean, cruel, and rapacious as they seem to be. We hesitate not to reply that the works in question are greatly the occasion of this, always keeping in mind, of course, the natural depravity of the heart, and the general intercourse of society trained in the peculiar circumstances of the Chinese. Their modes of thought and feeling, their social life and habits, are to be ascertained greatly by means of these lighter books, of which they are intended to be an exact representation, while they form a chief means of determining and confirming them.

The style of the Chinese language is very different in the written form from what it is in the spoken. It is highly artistic in the former case, and having been cultivated by a nation of scholars for hundreds and thousands of years, it has obtained a peculiar and finished appearance. The relation between the two may be described as similar to that which obtains between a work of art and a work of nature. The written form is properly of a laconic, rhythmical kind. The Chinese scholars love brevity and point, and in their best prose and poetry this is clearly perceived. We see a resemblance to it, in part, in the case of our own composition, and that of our ordinary talk. The language as well as style of the first of these differs in many respects from the second, and we find the principle carried out to perfection in the Chinese written style compared with the spoken forms. Of course the basis of the written language is the spoken medium in Chinese as it is in English, but the one is so different from, and so much more concisely expressed than the other, as to present a very great contrast indeed.

Attempts have been made by Missionaries to print in the colloquial style, but such works are despised by Chinese scholars, and the sentiments contained in them are treated in a corresponding manner. It is far from possible to find characters to answer to the words spoken in the *patois* of a district. The characters have been formed to express the written and not the colloquial style, and a sound in the latter has often no correlate in the written form. It is necessary, therefore, to take one of the characters of a merely corresponding sound to that intended, but which has no corresponding meaning in it, and this seems awkward and absurd to a Chinese scholar. He likes beauty, precision, force, and sense in the language that is employed, or in the characters that are used; and the style in which the book is written often goes much farther than the ideas that are expressed in it. When children are trained to read such heterogeneous productions as their native tongue in book language, they learn them, it is true, far more readily than in the proper book style. The reason of this is, that they are aided in the understanding of the printed characters by the apprehension of the sense contained in the whole, as in the case of our own elementary books; while the written style is recondite to the youthful mind, helping it in no wise to make out the sounds of the words, from their ignorance of the sense that is contained in them.

As to the original construction of the Chinese characters, they were no doubt pictorial or ideographic, formed according to the objects they were intended to represent. They were pictures of men and things, and they served this purpose for a time, but were afterwards found to be insufficient to convey all the images, physical and mental, that came before them in the increased intercourse of life. Hence it was that the later symbols began to assume a more composite and capricious aspect, resembling the phonetic or hieroglyphic forms on the Egyptian monuments. The characters as a whole are divided by native scholars into six classes, comprehending about 25,000 in all. The first is called *siang-hing*, that is, imitative symbols, amounting to 608; the second, *chi-sz'*, or symbols indicating thought, of which there are 107; the third, *hwui-i*, or combined ideas, of which there are 740; the fourth, *chuen-chu*, or inverted significations, of which there are 372; the fifth, *kiai-shing*, or uniting sound symbols, of which there are 21,810; the sixth, *kia-tsie*, or borrowed uses, of which there are 598. In the Imperial Dictionary there are 40,000 characters, which are said to be formed from, or to be a modification of 2000 symbols.

Whatever may be said as to the highly artificial and difficult Chinese characters, the fact is that they have been long and widely used. They are found sufficient for the literature on account of which they have been invented and employed, and we find they are capable of expressing the ideas which it is our purpose to make known among the people, in a remarkable manner. Each character has a variety of meanings attached to it, which may or may not be connected with the original or primary signification, and so a new sense may be imparted to certain symbols, when employed to express the technicalities of Western science and religion. In doing so, however, this must be definitely understood on both sides, and as much as possible a kindred meaning must be conveyed by the use of the appropriate symbols. Still we have a correspondence in the case of the Buddhistic literature, in which many characters are employed with a different meaning from the ordinary one, and also in medical and other native works, where the words do not bear the usual literary sense.

Some have inquired if it were not better to write the Chinese sounds in the Roman character, and so give a greater degree of ease and intelligibility to the whole. It has been done to some little advantage in certain quarters. The dialects of a few places have been rendered in this form, and some have been taught to read in it very fluently. But the employment of it on a large scale is impossible in present circumstances, at all events. In the first place, it is only the limited *patois* of a district that can be construed in this way, and each *patois* extends only to a comparatively small distance. We should require to apply and alter the spelling to meet the numberless variety of dialects that are found in all directions, and which diverge from each other greatly as we recede from any one point. It would necessitate a system of school teaching which it is not our purpose to undertake, and it would be in the face of all the prejudice and contempt that exist in the Chinese mind towards foreign things. Especially, however, it would not meet the case which the hieroglyphic characters now in use do to a wonderful extent. These were formed for universal service, and they suffice to do so, though they are difficult of acquisition, and require a capacious memory and a great application to learn the sound and sense connected with them separately, as well as to apprehend the ideas intended by them in combination. Yet there are untold millions who are trained and disciplined in this manner. They are to be found in all departments of social life, and are able to carry on their respective callings with varied degrees of attainment in a literary point of view. The result is, that by means of this common written medium or book language, they can communicate their ideas alike in all parts of the empire. However they may differ in their colloquial, their written medium is one and the same, like the Arabic notation, which conveys the same ideas in our own and other languages, though differently expressed in every instance.

With regard to the sounds of the written characters, though they are not exactly alike, when uttered by persons belonging to different provinces, or even in many parts of the same province, yet to a large extent their enunciation has a close resemblance everywhere. At the same time, though familiar to every intelligent reader on seeing them, they are utterly unintelligible even to the best scholar when he simply listens to their being read. This is owing to the great difference between the spoken and written forms. The one is addressed to the ear, the other to the eye. For the understanding of the former, there are many words employed connected with the main expression, that serve to fix the attention upon that expression, and give definiteness and force to it. From the comparative paucity of Chinese sounds, even allowing for their multiplication by the tonal accents, it would be almost impossible to understand which sounds and what ideas were intended in ordinary conversation, if there were no adjuncts employed that pointed out at once the sound or word and idea in question. These adjuncts satisfactorily avail for the purpose. There may be no essential meaning connected with them, but as they obtain only in the connection in which they thus stand, or rather, as they show in it the precise word in the clause or sentence, on which emphasis is laid, any inevitable mistake is thereby avoided. Language could not be carried on in fact, without these additions, that exist in the case of nouns, verbs, and adjectives alike. Even then it is sometimes necessary to signify in a still more definite form the word actually intended—to write it, in short, that there may be no doubt in the mind of the hearer. Persons from distant places, who can hardly understand each other, are often obliged to do this, and so their conversation is carried on.

There is great utility in the written medium, as it is intelligible to the millions of educated men throughout the empire. The style, like the characters, is highly artificial. There are great difficulties connected with the study of both. Four or five thousands at least of these characters have to be learned in their sound and meaning, while the recondite style in which they are frequently employed, enhances the labour of the student to an amazing degree. Still, the whole has its advantages in the circumstances of the case, and it is perhaps impossible to meet the requirements in any better way. The plan has served its purpose admirably for ages, and there is no reason why it should not be availed of in full measure in connexion with our Western sciences and religion.

Some urge the direct teaching of English to the more promising native students, and in this way communicate to them the higher information of an English education in the case of the Chinese. The present time, however, does not seem suitable for the purpose on any large or extended scale. The nation is not prepared for it, and in so far as past experience goes, it seems as if the combined study of English and Chinese were scarcely practicable. Those who have made great progress in the former have almost always come grievously short in the knowledge of their own native tongue. This may be owing to the circumstances in which they have been placed, and the temptation put in their way for mere secular pursuits. But we refer to the subject specially in the light of the supposed necessity of the English language, in order to convey in it clear and intelligible notions of Western science and learning. It is thought by many that the Chinese language must be unequal to express such notions, from its never having been employed in this way before. We can only state that those who have given themselves to the translation of the higher branches of Western science into Chinese, have not felt the inadequacy of the native tongue in any wise. The only difficulty is in the ideas attached to the native characters, according to the ordinary literary acceptation of them, being different from their necessary and indispensable scientific use. We find it to be the same largely in our religious nomenclature. The words and phrases suited to the occasion are there, but other ideas are usually applied to them than those intended in our case. The Chinese want the elementary training that would avail for the purpose, and so the same difficulty exists whatever medium of communication be employed. It is impossible to teach all the Chinese to speak and read the English language, and however difficult it may be for the foreigner to convey in a Chinese dress the science and religion of the West, the same difficulty would be felt by a native who learned English, and endeavoured to impart the knowledge connected with it in his own vernacular. It is the duty of every Missionary to apply himself to the utmost, in order to form an acquaintance with the Chinese literature, its character, its style, and its sentiments, so as to qualify him for high service in this field of labour. It is necessary with a view to his being appreciated by those around him, and however arduous the work may be, he will consider it as nothing, if it will only facilitate the great and glorious object before him. And it is no small encouragement and stimulus to him, that many have succeeded in this to a considerable extent, and have thus raised themselves in their Missionary capacity in the estimation of the people.

It is interesting to know that the Chinese literature, in its influence and diffusion, extends far beyond the boundaries of China proper. The native character has been largely studied, and is generally employed in other countries besides its original birth-place. In Japan, Corea, the Loochoo islands, Manchuria, Mongolia, Thibet, and elsewhere, it is more or less widely read, and books in this form are available in these regions to an immense extent. Thus our sphere of operation is vastly increased by means of the Chinese written language. Happily there are many facilities now at hand for the acquisition both of the written and the spoken forms. Grammars, Dictionaries, and easy lessons have been prepared for this purpose, and the difficulties that were once felt in the way of learning the language are now to no small extent diminished. The names of Morrison, Medhurst, Williams, Legge, Edkins, and Wade, are foremost in this department, as having rendered good service to future students, and their works deserve the highest praise.

In closing this chapter, we may observe that the practical influence of the Chinese literature on the native mind and manners, is of the most stereotyped and deadening kind. However the study of it may elevate above the ordinary standard of those round about, its whole tendency is to cramp and confine both the intellectual and moral energies of such as are engaged in it. They proceed in a given pre-determined groove, and are not at liberty to advance a step beyond it. All their ideas and activities are limited to a certain range, and they have no conception of anything else. It is theirs simply to revert to the past, and to find precedents and memorials for their observance in the future. This is carried to an extreme degree, and while it makes them thorough conservatives, no liberal influences and tendencies are ever admitted by it, into any department of social life. In mind and heart, in character and conduct, in their moral and religious nature, the Chinese are weakened, stereotyped and opposed to anything like change or improvement in the general condition of things. The language and literature of China, from the difficulty of their acquisition, and no less from their practical bearing on the native mind, are thus to be regarded as a mighty obstacle in the path of the Christian Missionary, and of the onward evangelization of the country.

CHAPTER III.

NATIONAL CHARACTER AND LIFE.

LOOKING at the Chinese as a whole, they seem to be a quiet, sober, and industrious people. They are naturally disposed in this way, and have no doubt been influenced by the training and civilization under which they have been placed for the purpose. Wherever we go, we observe these elements to be more or less the case. At the same time, the unity and homogeneousness of the Chinese in manners and customs, language and appearance, exist in connection with many local and provincial differences. There is a great variety among them, according to the part of the country to which they belong.

The Cantonese and Fukien people are generally of small size, but bold and enterprising in their habits and bearing. They are the emigrants of China, and are for the most part the class to be found in California, Australia, the islands of the Indian Archipelago, and in the ultra-Gangetic countries. Many of them follow a sea-faring life, and in the course of it are frequently engaged in piratical pursuits. Their ancestors are said to have removed at an early date from the original settlement in the north of China, and their departure from the pale of civilization is believed to show its effects upon them to the present time. Certainly they were the last of the Chinese who submitted to the reigning government. The natives of Che-kiang are in general milder and more refined in their character and disposition, and form in this respect an improvement on their southern neighbours. The inhabitants of Kiang-su are not marked by any special peculiarities. They lack force and energy to a remarkable degree, and show the natural lethargy and deceitfulness of the Chinese mind probably to a greater extent than any others. Many of them are distinguished scholars. The natives of Shantung, Che-le, Shanse, Shense, and Kansuh, are tall, massive, and strong in their physical structure. They are good traders in an ordinary way, more honest and truthful perhaps, but wanting in the tact and shrewdness of the Cantonese. The Honan race are athlete in their persons, and are regarded as in the first rank for political genius and strategy. The inhabitants of Hoo-nan, Hoo-peh, Sze-chuen, and Kwei-chow are looked upon as rather wild and uncultivated in their manners, but stand well in comparison with others of their countrymen. Ngan-whei and Kiang-se are situated near the former seat of government, and the natives are in many cases well-educated, though chiefly engaged in trading connected with the valuable produce of their soil.

Yun-nan and Kwang-se are farthest removed from the civilizing influences of the capital, and comparatively little is known about the people. The former province is said to have been subject for years to Mohammedan rule, and the mountainous districts of both places are largely occupied by the Miaou-tsze, or aborigines of China. It is supposed that they are the same as the Karens of Burmah.

The torpor and immobility of the Chinese mind are remarkable. These are elements indeed of the Oriental character at large, and arise, perhaps, as much from natural constitution, as from the training and culture to which it has been subjected. There was a time in Chinese history, when the natives seemed to be alive and forward in the arts of civilized life. Their language was in course of formation. Their intellectual energies were at work. Their material development was in progress. Their country was increasing in size and importance. Their religions blossomed and bore fruit after their kind. We may regard that time as the youth or manhood of the people. It was full of buoyancy and promise. But a change appears to have come over the land, that presents it now in a very different light. A paralytic shock seems to have seized hold of the nation. Everything that belongs to them looks as if it had the air of senility—the stamp of death. The progress and development of these early days have been strangely arrested. The Chinese retain their primitive peculiarities in a monotonous, stereotyped, and unimproved form. Their language is in chains, like that of childhood, notwithstanding the multiplicity of its sounds and the variety of its phrases. Their ideas of things are in general crude and puerile. Their views are never enlarged. Their culture and civilization are the same in essence and amount that they were ages ago. In some respects they have shown signs of retrogression, and appear to have no power to rise above their present depressed standard, alike intellectual and material.

What is the cause of this strange phenomenon? Can it be traced? We attribute it in great measure to the dominant yet deadening influence of the Confucian philosophy. This acts like the Aristotelian and scholastic systems in former days, prior to the introduction of the Baconian method, though in an intensely aggravated degree. The whole nation is formed upon it. All run in the same groove. No independent thought or feeling is ever exercised beyond the bounds of the prescribed course—the teachings of the ancient classics. The social life of the people is pervaded and determined by this line of things. Their mental conceptions are regulated and restricted by it. They entertain such lofty ideas of the person, character, and teachings of their venerated sage, that their only aim is to follow in his wake and study the books which are in general called by his name. The influence of these is absolute and overwhelming. They are sanctioned by imperial authority, and an acquaintance with them in the stereotyped meaning that is attached to them, or rather engraved upon them by the commentators, is the pre-requisite to all official appointments. Every deviation from this standard, every attempt at novelty or change, would be certainly crushed and fail in its object.

We need not say that this more than iron despotism is fatal in its effect upon the native mind and manners. According to it there is no possibility of advancing beyond the mark of ancient days. Its path alone is deemed right and perfect, and the nation has sunk down to the level of tame and listless acquiescence. There is no life, no energy, no idea of progress in connection with this system of things. It hangs as a heavy weight upon the necks of the people at large. They are earthbound, intellectually enfeebled, nay, paralysed in consequence, and until the incubus of Confucianism is removed we have no hope in reference to China. Water cannot of itself rise above its proper limit. Man is made greatly by the influences that are round about him. The Chinese have been moulded and determined by the literary and moral sway of their ancient sages. All classes have submitted to it, the learned and the unlearned alike, and that in virtue of the widespread education that obtains throughout the land. The scholars of China have almost absolute power. They are to be met with everywhere, and however ignorant the common people may be as to the letters and teachings of their native books, the supreme importance of these is universally acknowledged, and the national character and life of China have been fixed and stereotyped by them. In a word, investigate the spirit and tendency of the Confucian philosophy as it is everywhere taught and honoured in the country, and it will be easy to account for the pedantry and apathy and deadness of the Chinese mind in the sense we are now considering it.

It would appear from this as if there were a great and grievous defect in the power, energy or impulsiveness of the Chinese character. It seems as if it lacked stamina and force, and the general aspect of it is one of a low mediocrity. In consequence, the nation goes on from age to age in a very ordinary way. No great schemes are projected or carried out, as was the case in ancient times. Still it is wonderful that the affairs of such a vast nation are managed as they are. The machinery is kept agoing by the means that have long been in operation, and when the emperor or any high official manifests extraordinary ability, new and vigorous life is felt in all departments. It would, however, require a mighty impetus to be given in the right direction, to awaken the weakened and dormant energies of this great people, and there is little indication of it in the present condition of things. We have a high idea of the natural capacities of the Chinese, and believe them qualified to rise to a lofty position in the scale of nations. The materials are there. Their lethargy and deadness might be thrown off. They have become what they are greatly in the course of ages, and their attainments in civilization and culture, their intellectual, social, and political standing and character, might be advanced and increased to an indefinite extent. Hitherto the circumstances in which they have been placed have kept them in a fixed, formal, and antiquated condition. They have paralysed the force and energy of the native character, and repressed, as with an iron hand, any onward and upward tendency.

But what is the moral aspect and condition of the Chinese? This subject needs to be considered in the light of the teaching and culture arising from the Confucian classics, as well as from the natural habits and practices of the people. As we have seen, these classics are supreme in the estimation of the Chinese, and are taught throughout the myriad schools of the country. They exert a paramount influence in the formation of public sentiment, on all moral subjects, and in giving tone and direction to the conduct of multitudes.

There is one passage contained in them which may serve as an index to the whole. "What

Heaven has conferred is called the nature," that is the moral nature or conscience; "an accordance with this nature is called the path of duty, the regulation of this path is called instruction." The import of this Confucian saying is, that the will of Heaven is supreme; that conscience is its exponent or expression, which is therefore of the highest authority and obligation, and it is the duty of all men to observe its sacred teachings. These are to be ascertained in connexion with the sage-like instructions and example of Confucius. This is a principle to which all in theory submit, and the whole moral system of China is grounded on, and is an illustration of it. In keeping with it we have the natural relations subsisting between man and man, followed by a corresponding series of duties and obligations, which are urgently enforced in all manner of ways. Fidelity is enjoined on the part of the minister towards his prince; filial piety on the part of the child towards his parents; harmony and peace are to obtain between the husband and wife; brothers and sisters are mutually to respect and love each other; and friends and neighbours are to exercise confidence and honesty in all their intercourse and engagements. Benevolence, integrity, propriety, wisdom, and sincerity, are the five virtues inculcated for universal observance, and they are esteemed as the highest excellence of men. So far as these teachings are concerned, much may be said in their favour, and it is well that they should be so widely known and professedly appreciated as they actually are. We see them exemplified in the daily life of the Chinese to a wonderful extent; and we believe that it is greatly owing to this, that they have existed as a nation so long as they have really done, and in such an orderly and prosperous condition.

On the other hand, we are not to overlook the fact that all this fine teaching lacks one fundamental element, namely, a distinct and positive reference to God, as the supreme sanction and standard of morality. However dwelt upon in the ancient classics, it is now imperfectly understood, and heaven and earth only are spoken of in a vague and indefinite sense. We look upon this as a primary cause of the inefficiency of the Chinese morals upon the native mind; whatever may be said as to their excellence in a human point of view, they are feeble in practical application. Notwithstanding the encouragement given to their diffusion on the part of the state, and notwithstanding the high nominal appreciation of them among all classes, there is everywhere an absence of that clear and keen perception of moral duty which belongs to our Christian code. The virtues of truth, honesty, and integrity, may be recognised and commended, but they are far from being practised as they ought to be, in the common concerns of life. "The good are few and the bad are many," is an acknowledgment which they are all ready to make; and it seems to be only too true the more closely the social life of China is investigated. There are prevailing evils on every hand. Though the Confucian teaching in its appeals to conscience is far higher and nobler than any other heathen system, it fails in practical life to elevate and sanctify the depraved heart and habits of man. The moral character is feebly affected by it, and cannot be raised by such means to a lofty and dignified standard. It cannot suppress the miseries and vices incident to human nature, and make the nation pure, holy, virtuous, and happy.

We admit the presence and power of many excellent regulating principles in the country. We esteem and honour their application in a great variety of ways. We see on every hand a number of eleemosynary and other institutions, that are the fruit of benevolence and sympathy towards persons in distress. We have observed the working of these charities on a large and wide-spread scale, both in a continuous, systematic form, and occasionally when myriads of refugees were flocking around us, in circumstances of misery and want. We desire to give the utmost credit to the Chinese, for such illustrations of moral excellence as we find amongst them. At the same time the whole body politic is in large measure vitiated, corrupt, and depraved. Many of the worst vices obtain among the lower classes; and the higher, the ruling, the Mandarin sections, are cruel, unjust, and extortionate in their official life. Little faith can be placed in their word, and they hesitate not to break it, whenever their selfish and ambitious interests are supposed to interfere. Our political, mercantile, and missionary intercourse with the Chinese, brings out elements in their character and conduct, which may irritate and annoy, but need not surprise us. There can be no close, hearty association with them, on this very ground. We require to be always on our guard against the deceit, the dishonesty, the untruthfulness, the treachery with which they are chargeable; and their social life is marked by principles and practices, which place them in a low position as compared with our Christian civilization. Infanticide doubtless obtains among them, but we have no means of determining its extent. It is denounced in the criminal code and in other official announcements, but it is perpetrated in secret and does not appear in open day. The Chinese are aware of its moral impropriety, but excuse themselves on the ground of poverty or illegitimacy, or the comparative worthlessness of female children, or of the infant soul. A woman once confessed to me that she had destroyed three or four of her own girls, but she did not like it to be referred to, as there was evidently a sense of shame and infamy connected with it. We are inclined to think that the reports among us on the subject are greatly

F

overdrawn; but the fact is, there are times and places when and where the evil is more current than at other seasons and in other circumstances. Gambling is a prevailing habit in China, though it is declared to be illegal. Sensuality abounds, at times in the form of sodomy, but it is publicly condemned, and is not licensed and regulated as in Japan and other places. Opium smoking is rampant in all parts, and is eating out the vitals of the nation. It is the fruitful cause of many other social crimes, such as theft, suicide, murder and piracy, which are greatly on the increase, in consequence of the extensive use of the narcotic.

We cannot rightly estimate the Chinese character, without noticing certain other marked and peculiar phases of it. In the first place, there is the pride and prejudice of the Chinese, arising from their high ideas of themselves as a nation. It is a result of their education, their civilization, their culture. Isolated as they have been so long from the intercommunity of nations, and ignorant of the attainments of others in these respects, they suppose they are high in the vantage ground, compared with the rest of the world. They judge of those at a distance, from what they see of the tribes and nations round about, who are greatly inferior to them, and who have been accustomed to look to them with respect and honour. Their peculiar civilization is the very cause of their boasting and self-conceit. It is wholly their own.

It has been handed down from past ages. Their holy men and philosophers are looked upon as their great benefactors, through whose intellectual and moral influence they have been raised to their position of superiority over all other people. The literary class fosters this idea to the utmost, and as their influence is paramount it shows itself in this way even among the people. They appropriate all the supposed greatness and glory of their sages to themselves. They regard it as intended for and applicable to them alone, while the world at large is only to admire, and, as far as possible, imitate the wondrous spectacle. The inhabitants of other lands are considered to be most unfortunate, as living beyond the pale of Chinese civilization. They are not favoured with its bright and blessed illumination. We are in their estimation only barbarians, savages, white or foreign devils. Whatever may be thought of us by some who have had intercourse with us for years in various ways, the great bulk of the people, and especially the literary classes, know nothing about us. The general idea of foreigners is the same that it ever was. Our code of manners, our customs and habits, are different from theirs, and this is sufficient to separate us from them and determine our position in regard to them. It is not our actual standard of civilization and culture, but its contrariety to theirs, that fixes in their view our true character and bearing. Thus it is that the pride and prejudice, the bigotry and self-conceit of the Chinese scholars are unbounded; and while their ideas are of this kind, there can be no progress on their part in the right direction.

In intimate connexion with this, we notice a deep and determined aversion to anything like change and innovation in the country, and particularly at the hands of foreigners. There are many influences at work tending to produce this state of mind, that have to do with the past, the present, and the future. The Chinese believe in divination. It enters into every phase of their social life. Births, marriages, and deaths, are alike affected by it. The native almanacs are in great repute, and are consulted at all times and on all occasions. They divide the year into lucky and unlucky days, and determine the propriety or otherwise of any kind of work being done on these days. The feeling is so strong and universal, on this subject, that it would be deemed highly perilous to depart from the established rule. We hear on every hand of what is called *fung shuy* or wind and water, which means the harmony of nature, that may not be disturbed on any ground whatever. It has to do with the fixity and perpetuity of things, and stands in the way of all changes and improvement in the strongest manner. The direction of the graves, the building of houses, the most ordinary operations are regulated in accordance with it, and it is constantly alleged as an impassable obstacle to the carrying out of our Western ideas in China. Railways, telegraphs, the opening of mines, the making or mending of roads, and a hundred other things, are opposed from their not being in harmony with the *fung shuy* of the country; and both amusement and irritation are variously felt when this dogma is brought up and made to interfere with any of our proposed schemes. The literary and ruling classes take advantage of it in the minds of the people to frustrate our endeavours, and find it a convenient and powerful agent in the maintenance of their exclusive and conservative spirit. The people are threatened with all manner of evil consequences to themselves, their families, and even to the spirits of their departed friends, if the *fung shuy* of the neighbourhood is disturbed, and the foreign innovations are allowed. Still this *fulmen brutum* has been overcome in many instances, in the vicinity of our foreign settlements. Foreign gold has had much to do with the change, and would be effectual to a much greater extent, if the Imperial authorities would permit it. The native mercantile community and others largely avail of our steamers and sailing vessels, to the detriment of their own clumsy craft, and in their case other improvements would be welcomed if the superstition of the *fung shuy*, or "old custom," as it is sometimes called, could be done away with. As yet, however, we have operated little upon the higher and ruling classes, and until their opposition is overborne, we have small prospect of any wide-spread change in the general condition of things.

We may further observe, that the deep-rooted aversion to change is allied to an intense hostility to foreigners on the part of many. The one is a mere subterfuge in their case for the other. We are hated and dreaded. We have entered China not as friends and tribute-bearers, but as mighty conquerors, and independent of control. The authorities have been obliged to receive us, and cede certain rights and privileges which they would gladly take away if they could. Had they the power, the governing classes would soon compel us to leave the country, or confine us to some limited position on the sea-coast. And it is the opinion of not a few, that this is their aim and expectation. All they are doing now in the way of forming arsenals, building gun-boats, training soldiers, and manufacturing shot and shell, is only with this idea, that they may be on an equal footing with ourselves, and be able to fight on our own ground. In evidence of this, it is maintained that the Chinese authorities are more supercilious and overbearing than ever. They are strongly opposed to anything like concession to foreigners, and instead of advancing in the line of progress, showing that they are more favourably inclined towards us, they are actuated by a more exclusive spirit, and are resolved to keep us as much at arm's length as possible. The mission of Mr. Burlinghame to Western courts is represented by many as an illusion, designed only to ward off the day when China shall be thrown open to foreign intercourse in the fullest manner. Its promises of a liberal policy are said to be belied by the occurrences that are taking place in the country, and the stolid opposition of the ruling powers to the demands of our foreign ministers.

What is to be done in the circumstances? We are not writing for political purposes. We have other and higher ends in view. Only we may remark that it is indispensable we should maintain the rights we have already secured, and employ all legitimate means for pressing upon the people and the authorities, the necessity of progress in their national civilization and culture. We cannot be true to ourselves, nor to the country with which we are brought into contact, if this is not done. Any drawing back on our part from our just claims and privileges will assuredly be taken advantage of, and issue in our own discomfiture, as well as in loss to the Chinese themselves. This is the deep impression of the most intelligent men abroad, who are intimately acquainted with the facts of the case, and who are influenced by a sincere desire to promote the best interests of both countries. It is natural that the Chinese should feel towards us as they do. Were it no more than a sense of distance or estrangement in regard to us, it ought not to be wondered at. We are in the midst of them, as the thousands of Chinese are in California, Australia, and other places. Such is the contrast existing on both sides, that it will require a long time, and close and friendly association withal, before the differences can be broken down, and mutual confidence is awakened between us and them. There must be a correspondence brought about in the matter of a common civilization, or culture, or religion, and in this way only can we expect the estrangement, the repulsion that obtains in their case as well as in ours to subside. Much will depend on our treatment of them at home and abroad, for the accomplishment of this state of things. The manner in which we have dealt with the Chinese on our shores is no small indication of how they might be expected to deal with us on theirs, even allowing for the different circumstances in which we are respectively placed. At the same time, our path is clear in a national point of view. With a higher civilization at command, and with certain rights and requirements on our side, it is a moral obligation devolving upon us to illustrate the advantage of the one, and insist upon the observance of the other. We leave the course to be pursued in the interests of England and China to our political representatives. We presume not to dictate to them. We are persuaded that they know well the path of duty, which it is theirs to follow out, and though it is found to be surrounded with difficulties, at once from the novelty of the situation, and from the character of the men with whom they have to deal, we trust they will not shrink from it.

We are freer in the expression of our opinion, as it regards the bearing of the Missionary work, and the conduct of those who are connected with it. We hesitate not to say, that it is their part to be patient and forbearing in their judgment of the Chinese. This is a characteristic by which it behoves them to be marked in the highest degree. It is in accordance with the letter and spirit of their work, and considering the altered and improved circumstances of the present time as compared with the past, they may well be thankful on account of them. We believe, too, that Divine Providence is engaged in the conduct and direction of our great undertaking. It is not ours but God's. He is pledged to advance it in His own time and way, and it is our part quietly and patiently to wait all His sovereign will. Ages have passed away in which His cause appeared to make no progress, but it is otherwise now, and no impatience or complaining of ours will accelerate its movements a single step. Our duty is to take full advantage of the means and facilities that we actually enjoy, and calmly anticipate their increase in the onward course of events. The fact is that Providence is always ahead of us. The country is far more open, and there is far more encouragement connected with Missionary work in China than we have ever made a proper use of. In proportion to our ability and greatly beyond it, we shall find our opportunities multiplied on every hand, and we shall have no reason to lament the lack of occasion to make known the Gospel of Christ.

As the subjects of a treaty power, it is ours to be observant of the duties and stipulations enjoined by the international treaties, and not to imperil the interests or infringe the obligations on either side. It is true that Paul demanded his rights as a Roman citizen, and he was fully entitled to do so. Only he was perfectly aware of what these rights were, and they were acknowledged without hesitation by his bitterest persecutors. All we want is that the same shall be the case with us. Let us give no unreasonable offence. If we plume ourselves upon being citizens or subjects of England or America, we are not on that account to go beyond the proper limits, and insist on privileges which may not have been secured by treaty with one or other of the countries. We are not called upon to determine the import or bearing of that treaty in its original construction; but having ascertained its proper, its natural, its designed meaning, let us act accordingly, and if we exceed it, we are not justified in looking for defence or support at the hands of our respective governments.

This is our view of what Missionary policy ought to be. Though we do not sink our national character when we become the servants of Christ in a heathen land, yet in this sacred capacity we may not presume on special privileges in other respects, unless they are acknowledged by "the powers that be" to have been granted and secured to us. It is inconsistent with our profession that we should do so. It gives occasion to the enemy to blaspheme. It brings both us and our work into contempt, and we have neither moral nor national right to expect interference on our behalf, when we go beyond the limits that have been determined for us.

Over and above all this, however, we recognize the high duty and obligation of a Christian Missionary in a heathen land. Here we have the widest scope, modified only by the necessary circumstances of the case. It is ours to preach the Gospel in every place, following both the command and the example of our Blessed Lord. He acted out His own injunctions in the fullest manner. At times, He was withheld from carrying on His missionary work, and was obliged to remove to other fields, where He had greater freedom and security, until He knew that "His hour was come." When persecuted in one city, He fled into another. This is our rule and model. He has charged his disciples to act accordingly, and in the prosecution of their calling, to be "wise as serpents, and harmless as doves," and yet to "go into all the world and preach the Gospel to every creature." He forewarned them of trial and suffering in connexion with it, and this was abundantly exemplified in His own case, as it has been also in that of His most distinguished servants in every age. They are not to flinch from the path of duty on this account, though they are not needlessly or carelessly to rush into danger, as if they courted it for its own sake, or considered themselves martyrs in consequence. China has been the scene of persecution for Christ's sake in ample measure, as well as other parts of the world, and it may still be so when opportunity is presented for the purpose. We allude to this only to express the opinion, that a Missionary is not to be altogether determined by treaty rights and stipulations in the prosecution of his arduous work. He is actuated, we trust, by higher and holier considerations, though they have to do in some degree with his residence and labours in a heathen land. His motives arise from obedience to the command of Christ, and concern for a perishing world, and it is his to be prepared for all the obloquy, peril, and suffering he may be called to endure, from a course of fidelity to the one, and earnest regard to the other.

We have been led to make this digression, from the well-known condition of things in China. They are peculiar. They have not only a national but specially a missionary bearing, and as they are connected with the character and life of the people, it is proper that they should be considered in that light. Difficulties have arisen on the subject of Mission work, as well as on the ground of our being foreigners and aliens to the Chinese, and they demand a solution in the best manner possible. These difficulties were only to be expected when foreign Missionaries ventured into the interior, and exposed themselves to the consequences of doing so, at the hands of a people full of pride and prejudice, aversion and hostility. The question is, as to those on whom the responsibility falls in such a case. Is it personal or is it national? Let the limits on either side be clearly defined. We are persuaded that "offences will come," and they are not to be wondered at from the character of a heathen nation like the Chinese. We do not say that they arise from Christian considerations, so much as from merely foreign grounds, still it is the part of one and all in their respective places to do that which it is their duty to do. Let our governments maintain their political rights to the utmost, and show that they have both the power and the will to do so. This will intimidate such a treacherous nation as the Chinese are, especially in their representatives, from breaking their treaty stipulations with us, as they are always ready to do. Let our foreign authorities exert their influence for the enlightenment of the high officials as to our superior civilization and culture, and press these upon them in all legitimate ways. Let our merchants aid in the noble endeavour, as best they can, by the diffusion of useful information on the subject, among those with whom they come in contact. Let our Missionaries, too, act their solemn part in the matter; and by these various means we may expect in course of time to see the ignorant and stupid prejudices of the Chinese disappear. They will be taught to know us better than they have done; and appreciating at once our science and our religion, a new era will be inaugurated, and the long dark night of China will be followed by a brilliant and glorious day in the character and history of its people.

CHAPTER IV.

RELIGIOUS OPINIONS.

This is a subject of deep interest, as referring to the sentiments of the Chinese on matters of the highest and most solemn consequence. Without a just and adequate consideration of it, we cannot form any right idea of their moral and spiritual state, and of the difficulties in the way of our Missionary work. Our theme is necessarily of a complicated kind, as it is made up of differing and opposing elements. We shall have to review the course of these opinions from ancient times, notice the changes that have taken place in them, and determine their combined influence and effects on the people at large. We think it possible, however, to give such an idea of the whole, as shall enable our readers to arrive at a correct understanding in regard to it.

It is hazardous to form any notions of the religious opinions of the Chinese, apart from a direct and immediate knowledge of them. There are modes of thought and feeling everywhere current, as the result of ancient teaching and hereditary influence, that one can apprehend and appreciate only from having lived in the country, and ascertained from practical intercourse what the religious life and sentiments of the people really are. Having been in these circumstances for many years, we venture to speak freely and fully on the various topics now before us.

We shall refer, in the first place, to the opinions of the Chinese in regard to GOD.

In the earliest classic books, we find constant allusion to a Divine Being, bearing the name of *Shang-te*, or Supreme Ruler. Attributes and perfections are ascribed to Him, which are predicative only of the one living and true God, while there is nothing ever hinted of a kind derogatory to Him in this respect. Unity, almighty power, infinite wisdom, boundless goodness, supreme majesty, unerring justice, and the like, are excellences applied to Him on every hand, though of course it is not to be expected that there should be that clearness of meaning and fulness of detail which we find in our own inspired Scriptures. In virtue of such descriptions, however, it has been maintained by many that the Being in question is no other than the God of the Bible, as revealed in ancient times, and that this sacred name is a suitable appellative of the One Great Supreme. It is believed that monotheism was thus the original creed of the nation, and it in nowise opposes this idea that other beings were included in the worship and reverence of the Chinese. A wide and essential distinction is always drawn between the Supreme

Ruler and these spiritual beings, who were His servants and messengers, and were always addressed and honoured in a very different manner from the alone Supreme and Universal Monarch. This system forms the Imperial or state religion that is still observed in the capital, and the celebrated temple of Heaven is of great interest in this point of view. We regard it as invested with most sacred associations, which may have been forgotten by the worshippers in course of time, but which still cluster around it in the minds of those who contemplate its ancient institution, and rightly understand the services and sacrifices connected with it.

Another common appellation given to the Supreme Ruler is Heaven, which is employed with all due respect and honour, as an expressive emblem of the Being whose throne is in the heavens, and of which He was the acknowledged Lord and Master. The idea in this instance was originally the same that we find among ourselves, when we speak of Heaven in the sense of God, as more appropriate in ordinary conversation, yet no less distinctive and personal in the application of it.

A process of corruption or perversion of the original truth appears to have obtained in after days. The peculiar and personal character of God was gradually lost sight of, and heaven alone, or heaven and earth together, were regarded as the supreme objects of nature, and were spoken of accordingly. We meet with this as early as the days of Confucius. He employed the current language of his time. He does not appear to have given himself to the consideration of it, as he was occupied with merely moral and political questions. His example, no doubt, led the way to still greater deviations from the truth, and introduced that line of things which we find everywhere in China at the present hour. The idea of the Supreme Ruler in the light of the ancient teaching passed out of view. The works of His hands were substituted for Himself, and materializing speculations on the economy of the universe corrupted the ancient traditions contained in the first classic books, as to the Being, Perfections, and Government of God.

While this state of things was going on, other systems of religion came into operation, and extended their influence far and wide. Buddhism was formally brought into China about the year 61 A.D. Its founder was Sakyamuni, the time of whose birth in India is variously stated between the years 1030 and 560 B.C. He announced himself to be a moral and religious reformer, and in connection with his priestly, ascetical life, he became the head of numerous disciples. His system is professedly the transmigration of souls, in virtue of which human beings are represented as passing through an indefinite series of births and deaths, corresponding in their character and result to the merit or demerit of their natural lives. It is said that Buddha himself reached the state signified by that term—namely, enlightened, or perfect intelligence, after four hundred millions of transmigrations, and that all men are capable of rising to the same condition, by the same means that he pursued. There is no idea of divine, eternal existence connected with it. The only conception is one of unlimited advancement from the lower to the higher, from the imperfect to the perfect, from the conditioned to the unconditioned, from the human to the divine—the Buddhaship.

The other system is called Taouism, or Rationalism. It has been propagated under cover of the name of *Laou-keun* or *Laou-tsze*, who lived in the time of Confucius, and was visited by him in order to ascertain his peculiar doctrine. It was found to be far too sublime and metaphysical for his practical mind, and he left him confessing it to be so. Its object was the study of reason in relation to men and things—the mind and the universe. It was a highly speculative, pantheistic system, and recommended separation in thought and feeling and life from the engrossing cares and pursuits of the world. In after days, his disciples introduced many innovations, and borrowed largely both from the ancient and Buddhistic systems. Originally there was no idolatry or superstition connected with it, but it became notorious in this respect; and we find the old theology of China, as taught in the classic books, and illustrated in the existing state ritual, perverted and abused to an extreme degree. It is the opinion of not a few, that the idolatry of the rationalists is in the main a symbolic representation of the ancient religion of the country. The Supreme Ruler and the spiritual beings under him, have been idolized and placed in the Taouist Pantheon. They have the same names, and are said to fill the same offices, while they are believed to be an intended adaptation to the supposed wants of the people, which are not met by the more spiritual system of early days. This rationalistic theory has in course of time expanded and grown into a vast system of idolatry and superstition, that enters into almost every phase of the social life of China. The name distinctively given to the head of this Pantheon is *Yuh-hwang Shang-te,* or Gemmy Imperial Supreme Ruler, which is maintained by native scholars to be a designed representation of the Being spoken of under the old system, and by others to be the deification of a certain Taouist priest. However this may be, the common people on hearing the name Supreme Ruler, almost invariably apply it to the Taouist idol, as they have it constantly before them, and this forms a difficulty in the view of some adopting it for the true and living God.

In the twelfth century of our era, the materializing philosophy reached a culminating point. Certain distinguished men of this school flourished at that time, among whom *Chu-he* was pre-eminent, who devoted himself to the perfecting that philosophy and writing a commentary upon the sacred classics. In his commentary the allusions in the text to the personal existence of God were explained away, as synonymous with fate, order, reason, or necessity. Occasionally the ancient truth shows itself in his works, but their prevailing feature is atheistic, and a recognition only of nature in its constituent or primary principles as supreme. There is no eternal conscious existence in connection with it, and the whole resolves itself into materialism, as the cause and essence of universal being, and of which heaven, earth, and man are the three great ruling or intelligent powers. This is the system now taught in the myriad schools throughout China. There is no original or independent thought on the subject. The numberless scholars and teachers all follow in the same course, and take for granted the atheistic philosophy, and inculcate it upon their students. Though the existence and personality of God is a truth which commends itself to their reason and conscience, and admits of incontrovertible proof from many different sources, they are wholly unaccustomed to think about it, and simply talk of order or law, or the natural and necessary constitution of things, as a supreme and universal principle.

The common people have so far degenerated in this matter, that they speak only of heaven and earth in the sense of God. These express their highest conceptions of divinity, and sometimes appear to indicate a personal and intelligent existence in their view. Such is the bearing of their ordinary conversation, and it is very difficult to awaken within them clearer and more definite sentiments than what they have been thus led to entertain in the general intercourse of life.

There is no detailed account of the act of creation in the Chinese classics, but it is intimated or implied in a remarkable manner. Allowing that the terms God and Heaven are used convertibly, the operations or works ascribed to the Supreme Ruler can be rightly understood only in this sense. He is regarded as the author of all things, as causing them to come forth into being, as having at first divided the heavens and the earth, produced the lower classes of the people, and bestowed a moral nature on man. In the established ritual of the last dynasty, which gives definite expression to the sentiments of ancient times on the subject of religious worship, the creative power of God is acknowledged in the plainest terms. It is assumed as a positive truth, and the Supreme Ruler is spoken of as forming all things like a potter, and as the Maker and Parent of the universe. These ideas find a response in the bosom of every one, however mysterious the subject may be, and foreign to the ordinary course of thought.

Confucius speculated in some degree upon the cosmogony, and led the way to the most outrageous opinions. He speaks in the *Yih-king* of the "Great Extreme," which at first gave birth to two figures or primal energies of nature, and these in turn generated other forms, until heaven and earth, men and things, were all brought into existence. This "Great Extreme" has been regarded by Chinese scholars as the primary manifestation or cause of being, from which the present orderly arrangement has arisen. Subsequently it was thought necessary to begin the process with a more elementary principle, called "the Illimitable," to express the idea of immateriality or invisibility, as the source of existence. The whole system, however, contains no recognition of an intelligent personal Creator, and is an attempt to account for the general economy of things without Divine agency.

The popular or Taouist sentiment is that of *Pwan-ku*, as the first man, who is supposed to have been the original framer of all things. He is pictured as engaged in the mechanical construction of the heavens and the earth, with a dragon, a tortoise, and a phœnix at his side, while he is bringing rude chaos into shape and form.

Whatever may be the uncertainties in the ancient classics, as to the work of Creation, there is none as to the ways of Providence. This is acknowledged on all hands, and everything is traced to God or Heaven as the bountiful giver of all good. The course of the seasons, the productions of the earth, the continued existence of men and things, and all the phenomena of physical being, with the numberless blessings of social life, find their origin in the care and goodness of the Great Supreme. So general is this idea among the people at large, and so piously disposed are they in reference to it, that the simple utterance is readily responded to by all. "The goodness of the Supreme Ruler;" — "Heaven gives us all things;" — "We live on the bounty of Heaven;" are expressions on every lip, and though conveyed in a somewhat materialistic form, there is a great truth underlying them. The idols in the temple are no doubt prayed to for rain and fruitful seasons, but the Chinese in this instance even, have the notion of the supremacy of Heaven or God, while they think that the idols may exert a mediatory influence in their behalf. They are looked upon as in closer proximity to themselves, and as if more on a level with them than the Supreme Ruler. This we regard as a relic of ancient days when monotheism prevailed, and the *Shin*, or spirits of Heaven, were supplicated to interpose with God on their account. At present, the people are carried away by the Taouist idolatry and superstitions, which have grievously perverted their former ideas on the subject.

The Moral government of God is taught in the Chinese writings in the plainest manner. His name and attributes are used specially in application to this idea. Many passages might be quoted in support of it, and all classes are deeply imbued with the sentiment. Take, in evidence, the fact of conscience as existing in the human breast. It is said to be the gift of heaven, and the direct appointment of the Supreme. Its verdicts are in harmony with His decree. Nothing can exceed the sacredness and inviolability of this moral principle. It is one with heaven and earth, or God, in the estimation of the Chinese, and it was compliance with it that formed the perfection of Confucius, the sage *par excellence*, the equal of heaven, the divine man. Its sanctions are universally acknowledged, and all exhortations to virtue and goodness are based on the presence and approval of this inward monitor. The neglect of it or disobedience to its solemn teachings is regarded as highly wrong, and renders the criminal obnoxious to the punishment of heaven. It is to be lamented that God is greatly lost sight of as a personal and independent Being in this connexion, and that conscience is made to assume a paramount and supreme position. Heaven, earth, and conscience, are in fact the sum total of Chinese theology.

The active superintendence of God in all the affairs of life is acknowledged as a matter of the highest importance under this head. We meet with it abundantly in the Chinese books, and in the ordinary intercourse of the people. He is confessedly supreme in the history of individual men, dynasties, and nations. The character and conduct of kings and rulers are subject to His moral government. His approval or condemnation of them is shown in their appointment to office, or in the overthrow of their authority. Good men are rewarded, and evil men are punished under the immediate hand of the Most High. Warning counsels are given, public announcements are made, history is written, supplications and sacrifices are offered, and the entire sum of things is contemplated, under the impression that the eye of heaven is observing the whole. The idea of a just and inevitable recompense has a deep hold of the Chinese mind. Their proverbs and daily conversation as well as current literature bear ample testimony to it; and though the heathen gods may be looked upon and dreaded as the judges of conduct and the arbiters of fate, it is always in subordination to the will of heaven, of which they are only the exponents and executors. No system of idolatry has ever been allowed to supersede their natural, original, universal conceptions of the supremacy of Heaven, or of God, as the moral Governor of the world. These are elements that enter into the very constitution of their being, and may be used with great advantage in our Christian teaching.

Much is said of spiritual beings in the ancient as well as modern books, and in the general superstitions of the people. They are usually termed *Kwei-shin*, and divided into the spirits of heaven, the spirits of earth, and the *manes* of men. It seems that they were originally looked upon as real beings, and worshipped accordingly. The celestial spirits were the servants or messengers of the Supreme, analogous to angels in relation to God, or the high officers of government in relation to their prince. They were engaged in doing His will, and on being prayed to they were accustomed to descend to earth, and accept the sacrifices that were offered to them or their Divine Master. The terrestrial spirits were supposed to preside over the various objects of nature, and everything was believed to have a tutelary deity or spirit in connexion with it. The *manes* of men were the spirits of deceased ancestors, which from the earliest times received religious honours and sacrifices. The worship thus paid was at times collective, or as it is called to all the spirits, and at others of a more limited and special kind. The idea now mentioned of the two former classes having been regarded as real existences, appears to have been gradually abandoned, in accordance with the materialistic philosophy already referred to. The term expressive of the whole became an equivalent for the dual principle of nature, or for the mysterious operations and changes going on in the universe. The *Kwei-shin* were turned from a personal to a physical character in the economy of things, the one signifying the contracting, the other the expanding energies of nature. They began to take this place as early as the time of Confucius, and the idea increasingly gained ground in after days. Not that they always assume this position, for we meet with them often as intelligent objects of worship, in which capacity they are still honoured, apparently, in the state ritual. The most magniloquent expressions are made use of in regard to them, corresponding to what was thought of them in former times, and to the deification of all nature by the materialists of the empire.

The Buddhists and Rationalists have tended to reproduce the original conceptions of the Chinese on this subject. The spirits became in their hands real existences, and though ridiculed by the philosophers of the day in consequence of it, the fact is their ideas are more in harmony with the ancient line of things, as the intended personification of living beings — the veritable spirits of heaven, earth and men. The *Kwei* answer in this case more especially to departed spirits, from their supposed condition of misery in another state and to devils; while the *Shin* denote the natural spirits of heaven, and the more distinguished spirits of men who were elevated thither. The materializing of the *Kwei-shin* may accord with the speculative and pantheistic tendencies of a certain class, but it is contrary to the ordinary belief of mankind. It is easier to run into the farthest wilds of superstition and idolatry, than to change current ideas on this point, and transform the whole system of spiritual being into the mere energies and operations of physical existence. The divinities of China are the images or representations of supposed intelligent and conscious beings on the part of multitudes, while they are disbelieved in as such by the materialistic teachers and scholars of the day.

What are the ideas of the Chinese as to human nature and sin? These two points are intimately connected with the subject of religion, and they have been largely discussed in China. It is a fundamental principle that man is originally possessed of a good and virtuous nature. This is said of conscience, or the good heart, as it is termed. It is the gift which Heaven has bestowed, and obedience to it is the duty and obligation of every one. It is the basis of all right moral action. Confucius stated when near the close of his life, that he had attained after a lengthened process of self-culture to an easy and unconstrained compliance with its sacred teachings, and on this account he has been celebrated as the perfectly holy man. The common idea is that sin or evil is entailed by inattention to the good and virtuous principles thus characterizing our moral nature, and by the imitation of similar conduct on the part of others. The essential goodness of human nature is insisted on from the presence and operation of these right principles, and an appeal is confidently made to the inherent consciousness of all on the subject. The Chinese of course know nothing of what is called original sin, or the transmission of moral evil from our first parents, but they fully allow in connexion with the fact that man is born for virtuous action and with virtuous disposition—that there is a tendency in the case of other elements of his nature to gain an undue ascendancy over him, and so weaken or supersede the authority of conscience, that is, the will of Heaven in his heart and life. The actual condition of man is described in an elementary book taught in every native school in the following words. "Man at the beginning has a nature which is radically good. His nature is allied to virtue, but instruction is far distant." It is here intended to show the value and necessity of education. Its object is to bring the child back to his original integrity, which he is prone to leave even at the earliest period, by reason of innate and other causes. It is considered all important, therefore, to place in his hands the sacred and sublime lessons of antiquity, which contain the teachings and examples of the most distinguished sages; and in contact with them the naturally good and virtuous nature may be fostered and confirmed. The lack of this moral and intellectual instruction is supposed to be a leading occasion of the vice and error so prevalent in the world; and hence the encouragement that is given to it in the numerous schools that are everywhere established, and in the public examinations that are held with a view to literary honours and official appointments.

There have been scholars in China who contended against these opinions, as to the radical goodness of human nature. Such appeared to them to be the "evil imaginations" of the heart, and the corrupt practices of the life, that they maintained sentiments directly opposed to the orthodox belief. They insisted that the character and tendency of man's moral being were perverse and depraved, and that all the apparently good and virtuous elements connected with it were false and factitious. The adherents of the classic teaching admitted the general depravity to the utmost, but would not allow that any amount of it invalidated the constitution of human nature, as possessing right and virtuous principles, and as consequently framed for the purpose of illustrating and expressing them. Such are the views which now predominate in China, and in so far as the existence and essential goodness of our moral nature are concerned, there can be no doubt as to their truthfulness and consistency. We confess to the prevalence of the lower or the sensuous principles of the heart in every instance, and that they tend in great measure to supplant and overpower the rights of conscience. So prevalent are they that one under the awakened consciousness of them was compelled to say—"The good I would I do not, and the evil that I would not, that I do; for to will is present with me, but how to perform that which is good I find not. There is in me, that is in my flesh, no good thing. O wretched man that I am, who shall deliver me from this body of sin and death." These views are, we believe, in thorough accordance with the teachings of the Chinese classics, allowing of course for the increased vitalizing power of Christianity in the experience of its subjects. Evil is acknowledged in both instances, and so is good in connexion with our natural conscience, whether quickened or not by the special operation of God's Spirit. Its essence, its character, its object, its intuitions are the same in all cases, however much they may be suppressed or weakened or "seared." We have in this fact high ground to go upon in our moral teaching as Missionaries to the Chinese. They appreciate our representations of the good and the evil within us, the solemn obligations of the one and the unhappy prevalence of the other. At the same time, it is hardly to be expected that they should have those clear and impressive views of the "exceeding sinfulness of sin," which are peculiar to our Christian teaching. They are unable to apprehend the true state of the case, until it may be they are visited with calamities, which they regard as the judgments of Heaven, when they admit in general terms that they must have done wrong, or these calamities would not have overtaken them. Even then, however, it is difficult to make them sensible of the evil of their ways, or lead them to see that their neglect of conscience and their disobedience to the will of Heaven are sins with which they are universally chargeable, and which have incurred for them God's righteous displeasure.

The public services of religion in China are principally sacrifices, and the offerings presented are simply in the way of honour and duty, accompanied with prayer and thanksgiving. According to the established ritual these sacrifices have always been of a three-fold grade. The highest consists of the Border sacrifice or sacrifices, which are presented to heaven, or to the Power supposed to be ruling in heaven, in acknowledgment of His bestowing all the blessings they enjoy, and to Earth, or to the same Power as ruling in earth, and causing it to yield the fruits in their season. The one is offered at the winter solstice, on the altar of heaven in the capital, and is the most imposing and impressive. The other is at the summer solstice, though at times the sacrifices on these two occasions are increased to four or six, and at others are merged into one. Included in this first rank, are the offerings to the Imperial ancestors, and to the spirit presiding over the land and the grain. In the second class, are found the sacrifices to the inventor of husbandry, to the spirits of the hills and rivers, to the distinguished monarchs of former dynasties, to Confucius, to the standard, to the spirits of the sun and moon, and to the spirits of heaven and earth. All other sacrifices are of the third order. These services are by Imperial appointment, and are solemnly and statedly engaged in by the Emperor in person, or by his ministers deputed for the purpose.

On the part of the people, the first of these sacrifices is resolved into the worship of heaven and earth, which is observed in their own houses, on the first and fifteenth days of the month. In every household, the gods of the family are honoured in a peculiar manner. Their shrine is generally placed over the front door, and the object of it is to protect the family from injury, and bring down heavenly blessings. It is expressed in the form of a charm which is sold by the priests, and placed in a conspicuous position. The god of the kitchen is inserted in a niche, or pasted on the wall of that compartment, and is supposed to preside over the affairs of the house during the year. At the close of it, he returns to heaven to give an account of what has happened under his jurisdiction, and a feast is held on his account, that he may be pleased with the various members of the family, and be induced to report favourably of them before the Supreme Ruler of the rationalistic pantheon, in imitation of the more ancient theology.

The worship of ancestors is looked upon by the Chinese as of the highest consequence. . It has obtained from earliest times, and Confucius only confirmed it in the observance of his disciples. He said that he sacrificed to the dead as if they were present, and enjoined the services that had been appointed for the purpose. The practice is founded on filial piety, that we ought to respect our deceased ancestors as if they were still alive. At the time of ancestral sacrifice in the spring and occasionally in the autumn, the tombs of the departed are visited by their descendants for several generations, and various offerings are presented to them. The same takes place at home several times a year, in the way of worshipping before the ancestral tablet, or at the family shrine. The whole is done in the hope of promoting the happiness of the deceased, or of testifying the regard of posterity for their memories. It was formerly believed that the ancestral spirits had the power of benefiting and punishing their descendants, and it was needful to propitiate their favour by general good conduct, and strict attention to the prescribed services.

Many superstitious ideas and practices have been imported into the worship of the dead, for the avoidance of evil to the living, and the rescue of the deceased from suffering and want. Sacrifices are presented, prayers are chanted by the priests, and communication is professedly held by them with the departed, for the restoration of peace and quiet in the family.

This abetting of idolatry with the ancient system of national belief has gained for it a wide-spread influence, so that its priests are largely in demand in connexion with it. The offerings on the occasion are rice and other food, together with gilt paper in the shape of money, boxes, clothes, and various things, which are of no value whatever, but are supposed to indicate the filial piety of the worshippers, and are believed in many instances to be changed into the articles represented by them, so as to be made use of by the spirits of the deceased in the other world. It has been estimated that no less than thirty millions sterling are expended every year in this one form of religious worship, and it is so tenaciously held as to be a leading obstacle in the way of the gospel in China.

The worship offered in the temples of Confucius, Buddhism, and Taouism, is of varied interest and importance. The first is highly respected by all classes, but it is attended to once a year only by the mandarins, and some of the scholars in the district. Its chief design is to express their estimation of the character and influence of their greatest sage, who is regarded as the equal of heaven and earth, the teacher of ten thousand ages, most holy and perfect, and whose tablet appears in the temple surrounded by a multitude of others of similar kind. The inscription upon it is to this effect:—"To the venerated spirit of the holy man, Confucius." No idol or image is to be seen in the place, though the picture of Confucius is to be met with in the schools of the country. Very solemn worship, after the Chinese fashion, is engaged in on those annual occasions, with a view to honour the ancient sages and philosophers, though there is no certainty as to their present circumstances and condition. With regard to the religious character of Confucius himself little can be said. It was customary in ancient times to worship the spirits of heaven and earth, and entreat their help. Confucius was reminded of this shortly before his death, and was asked by his disciples for permission to pray on his account. The sage declined, saying, "I have prayed for a long time." We are left to conjecture the meaning of these words, whether they indicate the want of religious feeling in the man, or the want of any felt advantage in connexion with the act of worship.

As to the temples of Buddhism and Taouism they are numerous in all directions, and the two systems have multiplied and given form to departed spirits in a superabundant manner. These are frequently added to by the appointment of the Emperor, who has it in his power to elevate the spirits of departed heroes and saints in the other world, as he has authority in the case of distinguished men in the present life. In view of the numberless idols everywhere to be seen, it may be said that the whole nation is given to idolatry. The temples on a larger or smaller scale are to be seen in every place, and the worship peculiar to them is chiefly with a view to obtain present good, without denying that in some cases the future may also be contemplated.

There is no idea of atonement or expiation entertained by the Chinese in these various services. It never enters their minds that propitiation in the Christian sense of it is at all necessary, and the "offence of the cross" in this respect exists in China no less than it did in ancient Greece. The temple services, as performed alike by the priests and the people, are far from being of an interesting or impressive kind. The Buddhist priests are generally of the lowest class. In early days they were either orphans, or were sold or handed over to the abbots of a neighbouring temple by their parents. They have been trained to perform the various Buddhist ceremonies, and chant the prescribed ritual of that faith. They know nothing beyond these, and admit that they follow their profession only for a livelihood. There are very few of a higher grade, and hence it is they are despised by the respectable part of the community. The Taouist priests are little better in their character and standing. The ceremonies performed by the people are puerile as their offerings are paltry in the extreme, while they are grievously wanting in the necessary elements of religious worship. We observe nothing like deep moral earnestness and solemnity in their prostrations at the idol shrine, and the whole is little more than an affair of mere custom or form which they are satisfied with observing. Such are the circumstances in which they have been trained, and which they continue to follow as a matter of course, without any serious thought and feeling. All this may arise from the natural habits of the Chinese, or it may be in special relation to idolatry and superstition. The Confucian philosophy has greatly modified the influence of the current idolatry, and tended to produce a wide-spread feeling of infidelity and indifference about it. At the same time it is everywhere maintained, and its various forms and ceremonies are practised by untold millions of the people.

Notwithstanding the services that have long been performed on account of the dead, the doctrine of immortality and a future state was no part of the ancient creed. It is not only ignored, but dismissed from view by Confucius. A disciple asked him about serving the spirits of the dead, and he replied, "while you are not able to serve men, how can you serve the spirits?" The disciple added, "I venture to ask about death," and he was told, "you do not know about life, how can you know about death?" When inquired of as to the dead having a knowledge of our services, the master said, "If I were to say that the dead have such knowledge, I am afraid that filial sons and dutiful grandsons would injure their substance, in paying the last offices to the deceased; and if I were to say that the dead have not such knowledge, I am afraid lest unfilial sons should leave their parents unburied. You need not wish to know whether the dead have knowledge or not. There is no present urgency on the point. Hereafter you will know it for yourself." It is true that the sage could not be expected to give information on such subjects. It was therefore right in him to refrain from vain speculations, or pretending to know what he was really ignorant of. Hence he confined himself to more practical matters—to the duties of the present life. Yet the answers that he gave were vague and unworthy, and furnish reason for the scepticism and indifference that we meet with everywhere.

It was believed from the first that the spirit of man lived after death, and the worship of ancestors formed an unanswerable reply to every objection, far more convincing to a Chinaman than all the probable reasonings of Butler's Analogy. The state of the dead was one of utter uncertainty. It was supposed that good men ascended to heaven, and enjoyed happiness and honour, but it does not seem to have occurred to them what would be the condition of the bad. In the present life, personal rewards and punishments were allowed, and also in the case of posterity. The current opinions of the people are various. It is often said that at death all ends, and that the spirit is unworthy of being preserved in existence. It is also supposed that in the course of a few generations, the conscious being is maintained or lost in the memories or services of the living. The sentiment is expressed in this way, that the spirits of the deceased are bound up in their descendants, and if neglected or forgotten by them, the vital energy is scattered, while it may be retained by careful attention to certain sacrifices. The writer was once conversing with a person about the future existence of the spirit, who said that it was of such little value in his case that in a few years it would be dissipated and lost. What then was the benefit of ancestral sacrifice? He replied that it was the duty of posterity to offer it as an expression of filial piety, but after three or four generations at most, the spirits of the ancestors would be exhausted, like breath or vapour. Why then was Confucius worshipped for such a length of time? He said that it was altogether different in regard to him. There was a vitality, an excellence, a stamina about his spirit, far superior to the ordinary class, and as its influence was diffused all around, and retained in the memories and sacrifices of the nation, so it had lived until now, and was likely to live for ever.

In the systems of Buddhism and Taouism, a

future state is distinctly recognised, both in the way of reward and punishment. In the former, we have the idea of transmigration, according to which there is a process of ascent or descent in the scale of being, in harmony with the good or evil, the merit or demerit of the present life. This is determined in the other world, and the kind of birth that is subsequently to take place is often preceded in that state on the part of wicked men by untold sufferings, which are depicted in the literature and temples of the sect. The course of transmigration is indefinitely vast and prolonged. Millions and millions of ages may be required before the spirit attains the needful degree of purification and merit, when it enters into the state of *Nirvana*. This is described in the philosophic or atheistic creed as one of annihilation or unconsciousness, or cessation of all pain and pleasure, but in the popular understanding it denotes the happy kingdom of Buddha in the Western heavens; and this is the general sentiment in China. Buddha is said to have arrived at such a stage of exemption from passion or sensuality during his life-time on earth, as corresponds to the idea of unconsciousness or absolute rest and repose of the spirit. It had a moral significance in it, which resembled the physical state attained immediately after death,—one of deliverance from the joys and sorrows, the evils and infirmities incident to us in the present life. He was incapable of being moved by any of the sins or temptations of our common nature, and this is regarded as such a perfect state that it entitled him to claim the Buddhaship, or the highest degree of deified humanity. This same passionless condition of his body or spirit is presented as the standard of attainment on the part of all his followers. When it has been finally and fully reached, it will entitle the subject of it in like manner to enter the Buddhahood, and share in its endless felicities, whatever these may be. The tenets of Taouism or Rationalism are widely practised, and in the matter of a future state are a compound of various superstitions. Necromancy is a prevailing feature of it. The priests are largely engaged in rescuing departed souls from a state of purgatory or punishment, and raising them to a condition in which they become what is called "mountain men," corresponding to their ideas of the greatest possible happiness. These two systems are equally made use of in the case of deceased persons, who are supposed to be benefited by the merits and masses of both, in accordance with the payment that has been made on their account.

In summing up these details, we have to observe that the three religions of China are found in practical life greatly to influence one another. Though apparently different, they are said to have a common origin and end. Many Confucians denounce the other systems as foolish and absurd, allowing no sympathy to obtain between them and their own opinions. Others acknowledge that the whole are radically one in their character and aim. Virtue is declared to be the object intended and sought after by them all. The Confucians propose it by means of the learning and example of the ancient sages; the Buddhists profess it by the quiet and continuous contemplation of the life and teachings of their deified founder; the Taouists pretend it by the profound study of reason in its sublimest and transcendental sense, and the attainment of virtue is regarded as possible by one and all of these different means, The external forms and ceremonies of either system are admitted to be only aids to the realization of the same result, and it is of little consequence which is followed, if the final end is satisfactorily gained. Partly from this cause, and partly from the mutual interaction between the three religions in the social life of the people, they are to a great extent observed by all classes. They are looked upon as alike necessary and useful, and standing as they do side by side, each exerting its peculiar influence at home and abroad, they operate as a spell upon the country at large. They enter into every phase and element of public and private life. They form as it were an adamantine chain, with which the nation is bound, and from which it is impossible to effect its freedom. Atheism and Materialism, idolatry and superstition are believed in and practised at the same time and by the same individuals. The anomaly, the contradiction exists all through the Empire, and so amazing, so overwhelming are the difficulties connected with it in a Missionary point of view, that we may well be appalled by them, but we are sustained by the asseveration of the Bible, that the whole is to be overthrown, and China is to be emancipated, enlightened, and made happy. "Not by might, nor by power, but by the Spirit of the living God."

CHAPTER V.

THE OPIUM TRAFFIC.

We enter on the consideration of this topic with peculiar feelings. We may be accused of a degree of prejudice in the matter, and of giving only a partial and one-sided account of it; but we are not conscious of this being the case. We deem it necessary that the subject should be seriously looked at, in our survey of the moral and spiritual condition of the Chinese, and of the difficulties connected with any effort for their improvement. We are aware that they are charged with many evils of a social kind, that tend to debase them in the estimation of civilized humanity. But in allowing these to the fullest extent, as a result of their natural depravity and heathenism, we believe that their opium smoking forms a primary evil in their case, and a chief occasion of increasing and intensifying their other crimes. They are in this particular habit almost alone in the world. The practice is everywhere current. What is to be said about it? What influence is it producing on them as individuals and as a nation?

It is supposed by some that opium is indigenous to the country. We find the poppy mentioned in the Chinese herbal, and also the manner of preparing it for use it is thought as medicine. This is as far back as two centuries ago, but there is no indication of its having been grown or imported at an earlier period, or even for a long time afterwards, for the purpose to which it is now applied. It is known to have been used by the natives of Assam, and it is probable that in this way it was introduced into China, so as to have become an article of extensive native growth. It has been cultivated for many years in different parts of the empire, and there is reason to believe that it is in course of production to a very large and increasing amount. It has all along attracted the notice of the present government from the evil effects connected with it, so that earnest recommendations have been made for its suppression. We doubt not the high officials were sincere in their endeavours to put it down. Memorials are on record, couched in touching language, on the subject. The censorate has been employed in urging the strongest measures with regard to it; but from one cause or another, the whole has failed to correct the gigantic evil. The local authorities have often connived at the growth of the poppy, and as in other matters, found it more profitable for them to encourage than to prevent it. They are deeply smitten with the infection themselves, and the most inveterate and abandoned smokers are connected with the public service. We have no means of estimating the amount raised in various provinces of the empire. On travelling through some of the Northern districts where it was grown, we had striking evidence of its very general use. The appearance of the people bore sad proofs of its degrading effects. Those with whom we conversed about it acknowledged that the natives there were given to the habit in the proportion of eight to ten. The opium grown and prepared in the country is of an inferior or milder kind than that which is imported from India; like the native tobacco compared with the foreign article. It is cheaper, however, and more accessible in many places than what is brought from abroad, enabling the people, perhaps, to use it in greater quantities.

Foreign opium is said to have been introduced into China during the last century. In the year 1767, the importation had reached 1000 chests, and continued stationary for some time. Now it has attained a wonderful advance. In 1855, Dr. Medhurst drew up a paper on the subject, at the request of the Home Government, in which he says, on the authority of the China Mail, "that no less than 67,000 chests were delivered in China in the course of the previous year." Since then there has been a considerable increase in the entire amount, so that it is stated in the Missionary Journal of September last, as upwards of 89,000 chests, or 5,300 tons. One fourth of this quantity is taken to Hongkong, and the value of the annual importation is equal to about sixty millions of dollars. Here, then, is a vast trade engaged in from year to year with China, in which our Indian government, and through it all England, are deeply concerned. Let us consider the practical bearing of the subject, and what we ought to do in the circumstances.

We remark, that whatever some may say about the evil and mischief connected with it, the Chinese are thoroughly agreed on the point. It is looked upon as a great enormity, and as the cause of untold misery by the victims themselves, by all the well-disposed portion of the community, and by the Imperial government. We have never met an individual given to the habit, who would honestly and sincerely defend it for a moment. The confession is always made by opium smokers that they were enticed into it. When suffering from sickness or pain, perhaps, they were advised to use the drug, and it brought relief for a time; but they found themselves under a physical necessity to continue the dose, having neither the moral courage nor the bodily strength to give it up. Gladly would they do so, if they thought it could be done with ease and impunity. They dread the consequences, however, from what they see in the case of more impoverished victims, and from what they feel if deprived of it even for a short time. They imagine the cure to be worse than the disease. Were it possible to accomplish the one by any royal road, they would rejoice in getting rid of the other; but it is found very soon to obtain over them all the strength and tenacity of a confirmed habit. It gains entire mastery of the individual. The system is so inter-penetrated with the drug, and the craving for it is so intense and overpowering, that the victims of it are enslaved and helpless in the matter. The influence of evil companions also is said to be a frequent occasion of the practice.. Persons are led into it by friends and acquaintances, and ere long become equal adepts in it, to their own surprise and sorrow.

But what is the effect upon those who thus yield themselves up to it? Unless they have a sufficiency of food to fall back upon in connexion with it, they become physically enfeebled and emaciated to an extreme degree. So strong is the desire for it, that everything else must be abandoned for its indulgence. This is the case to an untold extent in myriads of instances. The Chinese, as a whole, are not wealthy, and the lower classes have a hard struggle for even the necessaries of life. Those of them who have taken to opium smoking, and their number is legion, make it their first aim and object, and it draws largely upon their small resources day by day. So long as they are under the influence of the drug, they are spurred on in the discharge of any work on hand; but when it has ceased, the demand for a further supply weakens their energies, and they can do nothing until it is satisfied. It is impossible to estimate the personal and domestic evils that are entailed by the habit in the case of its unhappy victims. Let those who have to suffer from it tell the wretched tale. We have seen enough to touch the hardest heart, and that might justly lead those who have to do with the trade, solemnly and entirely to renounce it. Not one word can be advanced in its defence, as if the drug were a useful medicine in certain cases, and as if its abuse alone were to be condemned. The physical and social effects of it, regarding these as even the lowest ground to take in the matter, are sufficient to demonstrate that opium smoking, like laudanum drinking several times a-day, cannot be pleaded for; and still less so if it becomes, as in China, an habitual and universal practice. In both points of view, it is a destructive and degrading vice, and affords no compensation in the way of personal or relative advantage.

But we specially refer to the subject on higher and moral considerations. The opium smoker is debased alike in his own estimation and in that of others. He has in every instance the conviction that it is an evil and a bitter thing. He knows it from his own painful experience, from the effects that it produces on those connected with him, and from the ideas entertained of it by the generality of his countrymen. He is consciously degraded by it, and its commonness or its long indulgence in no wise alters the facts of the case. Whether arising from this cause in particular, or from the influence that the use of the narcotic has upon its victim, there is no doubt that the opium smoker vitiates, corrupts, and destroys his moral character. It is deadened, seared, and perverted by the habit. It is a vice in the fullest sense. All who come in contact with the partaker of it are made aware of it. Under the stimulus or want of the drug, a man will commit the wildest and most atrocious deeds, or he will resort to the meanest and most cowardly acts, that equally lower him in the scale of humanity. He loses his moral balance by the habit into which he has fallen, and the bad qualities of his natural heathen heart are intensified and blackened by its means. Untruthfulness, deceitfulness, treachery, and cruelty, are the characteristics of the opium smoker, and to a degree far greater than in ordinary instances. No confidence can be placed in one who is addicted to it, and he requires to be carefully watched in all the intercourse of life. No real friendship can be formed with him. He has so debased himself in this way, that he is in fact a different man in his own eyes and in the eyes of others, from what he once was. If sin in any form has a deteriorating and debilitating effect, opium smoking proves itself to be "exceeding sinful" in this manner, and very few ever truly recover from it, or are restored to their original position.

It may be asked, what is the number of those who thus humiliate and degrade themselves? In reply we quote from an article in the Missionary Journal of February last year, written by Dr. Dudgeon, of Pekin, who has had large experience in connection with the Chinese Hospital there. In the main, it accords with our observations in other parts of the country. He says, "among small officials, 40 per cent. are opium smokers; merchants, 20 per cent.; of the followers, attendants, and male servants of Mandarins, 70 to 80 per cent.; of the female attendants of officials, 30 to 40 per cent.; of the fighting soldiery, 20 to 30 per cent.; and the same per centage among the literary class. Of the eunuchs in the palace there are 50 per cent., and one of that class who applied for relief told me there were over 3000 of them smokers, and that they had an opium shop in the *palace* itself. They lately set fire in this way to the Imperial Repository, which is just now being rebuilt. Of the reserve military force, 30 to 40 per cent.; of agriculturists and field labourers, 4 or 5 per cent., and from 40 to 60 per cent. in places where it is grown, as in Shansi. In Pekin there are opium shops in almost every lane and two or three in the larger lanes. Everywhere the poor people smoke in the largest numbers." The whole article is well worthy of perusal for information on the subject.

As to the practical effects of this social evil, we

maintain that the smallest participation in it is degrading and demoralizing. There are of course varied degrees of it. We quote from Medhurst's work on China's state and prospects. Judging from his own observations, he says, that twenty grains of opium taken habitually as the Chinese do, are sufficient to demoralize a man: and calculating the quantity of opium introduced in his day, it appeared that no less than three millions of persons were in course of demoralization at that rate. The amount consumed is often much more than that, but if the proportion is correct, in view of the vast increase in the number of chests now brought to China, we are warranted to estimate the persons morally affected and debased by it at fully ten millions per annum.

It is not ours to be the judges of character, or to pass a severe sentence upon the Chinese for their addictedness to this habit. But looking at facts, we find the opium smokers in the very lowest grade of Chinese society. In a Christian point of view, it is impossible that we can have any fellowship with them in our churches, or as converts to Christianity. It were a reproach and a stigma to our Christian name to do so. We meet with them continually in the course of our work. Not a few of them profess a desire to be connected with us, and some may have crept into connexion with us, but it has always been unknowingly on our part. If not reclaimed from the habit, or if they have again fallen into it, we can have nothing to do with them. The association of such men with us would be a snare to others, while it would be regarded with contempt and dishonour by all respectable persons. Christianity demands that the evil should be given up. We announce this as an indispensable term of discipleship, and must confess that the exceeding prevalence of the vice acts as a grievous obstacle to the spread of the Gospel. We are reminded of it on all sides. The smokers themselves charge us with having brought the drug into the country, and having ensnared them into the use of it. "Keep it away from us," they say, "and we shall have nothing more to do with it." The friends of such deluded victims, who have been called to suffer in consequence, bring it against us, and many others who see its evil workings in their native country. Multitudes are being ruined in character and circumstances by it, and we are told to go and convert our own people in the first place, that the means of their national disgrace and ruin may be averted. Such is our daily experience as Missionaries of the Cross, and the dilemma in which we are placed may be better conceived than described. Our countrymen often speak ill of us in the prosecution of our work, or of the unfitness of the Chinese to receive our holy Christianity, but they little imagine what a barrier they thus place both in our way and in the way of the heathen accepting the Gospel. We say it strongly and deliberately, that opium smoking is one of the chief obstacles to the conversion of the Chinese. It augments and intensifies every other difficulty, and its evil influence must be undone when any of its victims profess a desire to believe in Christ.

May we not here allude to the conduct of our own and the Chinese governments in the matter? We need not refer to the occasion of the first war, that it was owing to the determination of the latter to suppress the opium trade. Our merchants and others had timely warning in the matter, but it was unheeded, and the terrible calamity of war followed. Happily it has been overruled for good, so far as the opening of the country and other advantages are concerned. We have been benefited by it, and the Chinese ought to do the same. Only the conduct of the native officials showed what their views and feelings were in the matter. They persistently opposed the introduction of opium into their country, seeing as they did its baleful effects all around. We may not ask what would a European government have done in similar circumstances. One result of the war was that greater facilities were enjoyed for trading in the drug. It was still declared to be a contraband and noxious thing, and those who were disposed to traffic in it, had to do it at a distance from the treaty ports. We allow that in numberless cases the trade was connived at, on the part of those who were officially ordered to discourage or suppress it. The evil increased from year to year, but the government was never behindhand in denouncing it as a curse and abomination to the country.

The second war was commenced and concluded in 1860. The treaty on that occasion provided that the opium trade should be legalized. This was forced upon the Chinese by their English conquerors. It was considered desirable in the light of our foreign and professedly more advanced political economy, that a legal impost should be laid upon opium, and that the trade in it should thus be publicly recognized. The Chinese were compelled to accede to this arrangement, and from that time it has gone on in concert with all other departments. The Chinese officials regularly draw the prescribed tax, increasing it as usual when away from the treaty ports. The whole affair, however, is acknowledged to be vicious and vile. The government now and again denounces it, threatening all manner of pains and penalties on those connected with the administration, if they partake of it, and counselling the people at large to abstain from it, as a pernicious and poisonous drug. Some doubt their sincerity in these edicts, still the fact is that they are issued, and all classes are thoroughly convinced that opium is impoverishing, degrading, and ruining the empire. We cannot expect the same view of things to obtain in China as among ourselves, in regard to the interests of their country, or as to the course they ought to pursue in the circumstances, but it is certain that the Chinese look upon the opium trade as an evil introduced amongst them by foreigners, and that it is carrying death and destruction along with it. They may be powerless in suppressing it, but that the well-disposed portion of the people, forming in this respect the great majority, would rejoice in the suppression of it, is a matter that no one can deny. It would raise us highly in their estimation, and go far to abate the hostility and aversion felt towards us in all parts of the country. We are identified with the traffic. We are charged as the occasion of all the mischief and evil attached to it; and were we to relinquish it altogether, publishing the fact far and wide, it would vastly redound to our credit and advantage in their estimation, and be a blessing to the country at large.

We venture to ask, is the opium trade necessary, honest, Christian, in any sense whatever? Can we righteously and conscientiously participate in it? Can we engage in a thing which is in no wise productive of good, and is the direct and acknowledged cause of much evil to the Chinese? They confess that they are befooled and besotted by it. In their own persons, in the various relations of life, in their national character and capacity, they have been overcome, enslaved, degraded by it. They will not defend the use of it in any instance, except that having betaken to it, they cannot give it up.

The abandonment of the trade would be confusing for a time to our mercantile interests, to our Indian exchequer, and to the myriads who have become its victims. What then? That is no argument for its continuance. And the call is loud and earnest to those who have anything to do with it. Be the consequences what they may, in any of these respects, the duty of all Christian men is to have no connexion with it. We know there are several honourable firms in China who have wholly abstained from the traffic. They are honoured accordingly, but there are many whose names and hands are soiled with the drug. We know one gentleman who was so thoroughly convinced of the evils of the trade, that he wrote on his own authority to Bombay to cease the consignment of any more opium to his house, and he was prepared to stand by it, however he might be called to suffer. What should hinder all our English and American merchants following his example? What should prevent an arrangement with the Chinese authorities that would put a stop to the traffic entirely, in so far at least as they are concerned, though it might be the occasion of smuggling on the part of unprincipled individuals? Let it be so rather than we should participate in the evil thing. We are persuaded that our Christian merchants, on the calm and serious consideration of the subject, would readily see the mischief arising from it, and be induced to abandon it. Were it so, China would in a short time present a different appearance from what it does. Led by necessity to give up what is now so freely circulated in the country, and finding that they were a thousand times better without it, all classes would be excited to a deeper interest in our Western science and religion, than they can possibly be while saturated and debased by the opium that they receive at our hands.

In closing these observations we would make one reflection more. How is it that Christian Englishmen should be the means of trading in such a commodity as opium with the Chinese, in exchange for their most useful and valuable produce? Their connexion with us is honourable in a high degree, and they have mightily the advantage of us in this respect. Our country has been immensely benefited by the enlarged introduction of such articles, as silk and tea, "the cup that cheers, but not inebriates." We are indebted to the Flowery Land in this matter, to an extent of which we can form no adequate idea. The truth is, that there are few countries and few people to which and to whom we are under higher obligations, in a commercial and civilizing point of view. Our whole social life has been revolutionized and advanced by what has been brought to us from the Middle Kingdom. And what have we carried thither in return for these commodities? What are we doing to make their social life similarly happy and comfortable, to entitle us to their respect, and to promote their well-being and prosperity? Let the article under consideration furnish a reply—an article which we should consider ourselves demeaned, dishonoured and ruined by using in the manner, and for the purpose for which we know they do it. Neither we nor any other civilized government would tolerate the conduct, which we have shown to them, were it in our power to resist it and carry out our similar prohibitions of the accursed thing from our native shores. While they have fostered the elements of our high civilization, while they have met our demands in a way that does them credit, and that enhances our comforts and enjoyments in a form similar to their own, we have introduced and encouraged elements among them that have only debased and impoverished them, and all in direct opposition to what we think right and proper for ourselves.

Talk of the degeneracy and low character of the Chinese! What has been the means of producing it, perhaps, more than anything else? Ask themselves. Their universal answer is—opium. And who are the guilty parties in the matter? We Christian Englishmen. They have acted towards us nobly and well in aiding, elevating, and improving our civilization. We have acted towards them in a manner, which has lowered, degraded, ruined them, in soul and body, individually and nationally, to a far greater extent, probably, than any of their other propensities and habits. It is of no use to plead that it is their own fault. We profess to regard them as children, and sometimes wish to treat them as such, in our international policy. Would that it were so in the present instance. The trade in question is injurious beyond expression. As children the Chinese find it impossible to resist it. Let us withhold it from them, as they themselves entreat us to do, and prosecute our trade with them in things that shall prove honourable to ourselves and beneficial to them. We can never equal them in the value of our products, but we have a civilization, a culture, a science and a religion in our possession, the communication of which will amply compensate them for what they are able to give to us in a material point of view. Let us rise to a proper sense of our duty in this respect, and there will be no surer means in our estimation, for promoting the best interests of humanity in China, than by abandoning a traffic which is fraught only with evil and mischief. Let us convince the Chinese of our honourable, upright, and Christian character in this matter, and we shall soon find them ceasing in their opposition to foreigners, and in their abhorrence of us in every sense of the term. In a word, let us give them the best and most useful things that we have at our disposal, and not the worst and most pernicious and degrading, like for like, worth for worth, and there will be ground for their appreciation of us, as at least on an equality with themselves.

CHAPTER VI.

MISSIONARY WORK.

When Christ gave the command to his disciples to "go into all the world, and preach the gospel to every creature," there was the dawn of a new era in the history of the human race. The meaning of the commission was far from being fully apprehended by those to whom it was announced, and they required higher qualifications than they possessed at the time, to enable and constrain them to carry it out. The promise of the Father, however, was duly fulfilled in them; and under the teaching and influence of the Holy Spirit, they were led as circumstances called them to convey the message of salvation to the ends of the earth. We are familiar with the early proceedings of the Christian Church; how that from Jerusalem the word of the Lord was sounded abroad far and wide. By one means and another, by chosen apostles and private individuals, the good news was carried to distant and remote places, till in the process of time, Christianity gained multitudes to its side, and became the recognized religion of the conquerors of the world.

But all this was confined to parts that were comparatively well known, and more or less connected with Western civilization. We need to look forward in the course of years to observe the progress of the Gospel in the country we are now contemplating. There was little or no contact with it in the first ages of Christianity, and yet we find that the light of truth spread thither at an early period, so that in the year 300, Arnobius speaks of its effects among the Seres or Chinese, the Persians and Medes. Monks returned from the country with the eggs of the silkworm in 552. They had resided there for a long time, and were probably not the first who had done so. Chinese history, too, contains the account of the arrival of certain priests from Tatsin or Judea, who had appeared at court and been approved by the Emperor, so as to warrant the propagation of their religion. This was during the reign of Tatsung, in 639. We might have known little more about the matter, had it not been for an important discovery in 1625 of a stone tablet in Si-ngan-fu, in the province of Shen-si. There was an inscription upon it in Chinese and Syrian characters, which professed to be a narrative of the diffusion of the Kin-kiaou, or the illustrious religion of Tatsin, that is Christianity, in China. It is the most ancient Christian record of the kind in Asia, and is highly valuable on its own account. The date of its erection is stated to be 781, and there can be no doubt as to the genuineness of it. The tablet is still in the same place, and has been verified of late years by Protestant Missionaries, as it was first discovered by Roman Catholics. It was the work of Nestorian Christians, who are supposed to have entered the country as early as the year 505, A.D. They seem to have prospered for a long time, and the tablet gives a full account of their mission, its character and successes in different reigns. They appear to have gradually disappeared from public view, and with the exception of the above tablet, we have no further trace of them.

The first Romish missions began about the latter part of the thirteenth century, when the Nestorians were in existence, who opposed them both in central Asia and in China. They made considerable progress, but suffered much during the defeat of the Mongols and the rise of the Ming dynasty, and seem to have been extinguished altogether. In 1552, the celebrated Francis Xavier contemplated a mission to China, and was actually on his way to it from Goa, when he died in sight of the country. The next Missionary of note who reached it after his day was Matthew Ricci, in 1581, when he established himself at Canton. He was a man of high scientific attainments, and in the prosecution of his work, he went to the capital through the interior of China. He soon became famous, from his mathematical and astronomical knowledge; and the Emperor desired him to send for a number of able men to assist in the Observatory and other departments. Many European scholars of this class soon joined him, who added greatly to the celebrity of the Mission. While they were engaged in the capital, others were occupied in the provinces, spreading their religion. Multitudes joined their ranks and became converts to the faith. Changes, however, occurred in the course of events, chiefly in consequence of the differences that arose between the Jesuit and the other Missionaries. The progress of the faith was arrested, and its prospects were blighted; the Emperor was offended, and persecution commenced. He expelled the priests to Macao, and the Catholic religion was strictly forbidden. After that time, the work was carried on under many disadvantages. Its emissaries were obliged to conduct their operations in a most secret manner, and were exposed to many cruelties if found in the interior by the local authorities. They claim, however, to have been able to maintain their missions in different parts of the country, during the long night of trial; and the number of their converts is said to amount, at the present time, to upwards of half a million.

It was in 1807 that the London Missionary Society sent out the Reverend Robert Morrison to China. He was the first Protestant Missionary to that part of the world. He commenced his work in the neighbourhood of Canton, where the foreign merchants were residing, and persevered in it in a manner that does him the highest credit. From the interdict laid upon foreigners going into the interior, he remained at his post, acquiring the language, and laying the foundation of Protestant Missions in China. The sentence of exclusion lasted long, and was rigorously observed by the authorities. Though Merchants and Missionaries increased in number, and our intercourse with China was greatly advanced, no improvement took place in the way of extended facilities. Each year seemed to add to the disadvantages of trade and commerce; while, as there was no possibility, so there was no inducement, for Protestant Missionaries to penetrate into the interior. It was otherwise with the Romanists, who had converts in various places, and who were welcomed by them wherever they went. Still the first Missionaries, though confined to a particular locality, were not idle. They worked for the future, as they sowed the seeds of Divine truth in their immediate neighbourhood. They had large scope for this purpose, by their being in the vicinity of numbers of people, who could hear the word and receive religious books for themselves and for transmission into the country. They could do no more. They were called to wait till, in the Providence of God, the door was opened, and they were at liberty to go into other places and preach the gospel.

That time came at the conclusion of the first war with China, in 1842. In virtue of the treaty then made, five ports were opened for foreign trade, and Hongkong was ceded to us as British territory. Means were at once devised to occupy these ports by various Missionary Societies in England, Germany, and America. The arrangement was hailed as a blessing from heaven. Though the places were partly known before, and were chosen in view of their adaptation for commercial purposes, they were regarded as of special interest and importance in a Missionary point of view. The openings brought us into contact with the people to an immense extent. Each of the ports, — Canton, Amoy, Fuchow, Ningpo, and Shanghai — had a vast population, and formed avenues to the interior, of which we hoped in time to take advantage. We were at liberty to labour in these places, with the exception of the first, in the freest and fullest manner. No special difficulty was found connected with them, beyond the natural feeling of estrangement from, and fear of, foreigners in the minds of the Chinese. Years passed on in this way, during which we enjoyed the greatest facilities and much encouragement in carrying on our work. At most of the ports we gradually went beyond the bounds prescribed, and found the inlying country offering splendid opportunities for Missionary work. We became familiar with the towns and cities at the distance of at least a hundred miles in various directions. This added immensely to our field of labour, and though exposed to a degree of peril at the outset, from the ill-will of some of the people, the reception we met with on the whole was of a gratifying kind. It was impossible to estimate the amount of population thus brought within our reach, and each year seemed to add to it by the extension of our itinerant labours, and our increased acquaintance with the country.

But it was not intended that we should rest in the enjoyment of even these facilities, great and growing though they were. In 1858, it was resolved by the English government to demand a revision of the first treaty, with an apology for certain grievances that had occurred in the South, and also that further privileges should be enjoyed, more especially that the English minister should reside in the capital, and come into direct communication with the Chinese authorities. On this being refused, the Taku forts were taken, and the Chinese army was driven back, when the treaty of Tientsin was concluded, fully allowing the various concessions that were asked. Next year, on the English ambassador proceeding to the capital, he was opposed at Tientsin. It had been strongly fortified, and on attacking it we were repulsed. In 1860, the English and French forces took the place and moved on to Pekin, encountering the Chinese army at different points, till they dictated terms of submission to the Imperial plenipotentiaries. The new treaty was duly signed, and provided all that was required. It was arranged that the English minister should reside at the capital, and that other ports should be opened on the same conditions as the others. It was arranged too, that passports should be issued at the Consulates, entitling us to travel through the land for pleasure, trade, or otherwise. Swatow in the south, Tĕngchow, Tientsin, and Newchwang in the north, Takao and Taiwan in Formosa, Keungchow in Hainan, and sometime afterwards Chinkeang, Kiukeang and Hankow on the Yangtze, in the central part of the empire, were thus added to the places previously secured to us. This increased our facilities amazingly. The country was opened to an extent of which we had formed no conception, and we acknowledge the hand of Providence in it all.

These places with a few exceptions were found to contain a vast population, while they furnished the means of getting into the interior, which greatly enhanced their value and importance. It was not to be expected that all our difficulties and dangers were thus cleared away, or that the people were everywhere prepared to receive us in a cordial spirit. The legal opening of the country did not allay their national pride and prejudice, or their feelings of aversion and hostility to foreigners. This was an obstacle to be overcome gradually, and we were forewarned of peril and inconvenience of various kinds. Such was soon found to be the case, but after all it was not to be wondered at. The character or disposition of the natives, and especially of the ruling and literary classes, was in no wise altered by the arrangements of the treaty. Their enmity and opposition were ever ready to break out, and place the foreigners in circumstances of trial or danger. Painful instances of this kind have frequently occurred, and life has been lost in connexion with them. It will require a long time and extended intercourse between the Chinese and ourselves, before all their national antipathy and jealousy subside, and they are found ready in all parts of the country to receive us amongst them. Still much has been done in this way, to an extent indeed that may well astonish us, and we are persuaded that in the course of events the ill-will and prejudice of the people will be subdued, and we shall be admitted everywhere on equal terms. Our conduct at the ports, and our journeys into the interior will be helpful in the attainment of this result. At the outset we were independent strangers. The natives were timid and hostile, and fearing that our presence would be injurious to their interests, they seemed to feel justified in treating us as enemies. They had not been accustomed to the sight of foreigners. They had heard the most outrageous and malicious stories about us, but when they found there was no ground for such things at all, their opinions underwent a happy change. We were able gradually to move about in a free and open manner, and thus our tours have been extended over hundreds and even thousands of miles. The country has been traversed from Canton to the Great Wall, and in other directions immense distances have also been gone over. Always allowing for a degree of hazard in connexion with these journeys, still it is the case that the difficulty is not so much in travelling as in settling down in an interior district. The thing is novel in the view of the natives, and the attempt on our part awakens all their old prejudice and opposition, so as to render it often a difficult and dangerous experiment, that requires to be carefully and prudently dealt with.

Here it may be proper to make a few remarks on the terms and bearing of the treaty in this respect. Does it warrant our settling down in all places, and have we a right to demand this privilege wherever we like? If it be so, what is to be said of the late troubles in China on this very ground, and which are of the same nature with what has occurred elsewhere? We quote from the *North China Herald* of 16th February, 1869, on the subject. It states that a request was made by the Shanghai Chamber of Commerce to Lord Elgin, for liberty to travel and reside in the country and in the inland towns of China. The writer goes on to say:—" It is interesting to read anew by the light of this request, the article of the Tientsin treaty, authorizing British subjects to travel in the interior. The omission from the latter of the word 'reside' can hardly have been accidental. At any rate permission to travel only for purposes of pleasure or trade was granted, and three ports only on the Yangtze were opened."

This we always understood to be the original meaning of the treaty, and so far it was acted on till lately. Whenever Missionaries attempted to settle in the country, they considered it was at their own risk, and that they could not be legally sustained. The French treaty secured the liberty of settling in the interior to the Roman Catholic Missionaries, and as we have the favoured nation clause in ours, it was presumed that we had a similar right thereby ceded to us, and that as Missionaries we were justified in establishing ourselves in the country wherever we pleased. Some assert that the clause in question has not been taken up by our Home Government in the Missionary view of it, and that our authorities do not hold themselves responsible for the consequences of any one acting upon it. Be this as it may, the thing was tried and the history of the late troubles at Yangchow is fraught with instruction on the point. If we are to ground our right in the matter upon the terms of the French treaty, in connexion with our own favoured nation clause, it is desirable that our Government should declare itself accordingly. For the time being, it has taken the very opposite course, and the statements of a certain member of the House of Lords are notorious for their vilification of Missionaries, in language, sentiment and spirit that are highly unbecoming. It is not to be wondered at that people at home should be ignorant of the facts of the case in China, we mean of the real feelings of the people, and the possibility and necessity of progress. So far as our Government is concerned, we are deeply impressed with its obligation neither to force nor to relinquish the plea of full international communication. Be the obstacles what they may, enlightened civilization demands the freest intercourse, conformably to the laws and regulations that arise out of it. We cannot assume that such enlightenment exists in China, but it is our part to hasten it on by all legitimate means. We are thankful for the facilities and opportunities that are already enjoyed in Missionary work. They are far from having been taken full advantage of, yet such is the effect of our foreign connexion with China, that all the advantages of late years are found and felt to be only stepping stones to further and greater acquisitions. Our cause is necessarily onward. The peculiar circumstances of the case in a mercantile and Missionary point of view require increased facilities, and wider scope for our operations. It is impossible to be satisfied with past attainments, and it is well that our national spirit and Christian zeal should lead to the demand for more extended intercourse, for the breaking down of every needless restriction, and for the universal opening of the country. The wish, the aim are prelusive of the result. Only let us be faithful to our duty in the earnest, enlightened, appropriate agitation of the question, and one day we shall wake up to the full realization of it. Meanwhile we would endeavour to disabuse the minds of friends at home, as to any idea of impossibility in the matter, or as if the object contemplated were too formidable to be attained in the present condition of things. The prejudice, bigotry and aversion to foreigners existing especially among the ruling and literary classes, and in measure among the common people, admit of a remedy in time, and much will depend upon our conduct in the matter. We would urge unswerving persistency on the part of our authorities in their representation of the subject to the Chinese government, and thorough Christian propriety in all the movements of our Merchants and Missionaries, as the best means of bearing down the native opposition. We are satisfied that in so far as the end in view is a right one, it will in due course be attained, despite all the difficulties at present connected with it.

But our topic requires that we should notice the Missionary work that has actually been done in China, in consideration of the facilities that have of late years been enjoyed.

We would refer, in the first place, to the translation of the Scriptures as a matter of high importance. Dr. Morrison gave himself to this task as soon after his arrival as possible, and was subsequently aided in it by Dr. Milne. As the first work of the kind, and accomplished in circumstances very different from those now existing, it deserves very great commendation indeed. It was published and circulated widely. When the country was opened and the Missionaries increased in number and efficiency, it was deemed needful that a revision or new translation of the New Testament should be made. A Committee of Delegates was appointed consisting of representatives from different Missionary Societies, English and American, which began its labours in Shanghai in July, 1847. The Rev. Drs. Medhurst, Bridgman, and Boone, with Messrs. John Stronach and Walter Lowrie, were the members of that Committee. The latter lost his life soon after at the hands of pirates, while crossing the Hang-chow bay on his way to Ningpo, and Bishop Boone was withheld engaging in the work by his infirm state of health. In about two years the work was finished. It was a scholarly production, clear and idiomatic in its style, as well as a faithful translation of the Scriptures into the Chinese language. In view of the high qualifications of the translators and the great unlikelihood of obtaining the services of such men for a long time to come, it was resolved to continue the work by the similar translation of the Old Testament. The Rev. William Milne was added to the Committee, and the work was carried on successfully. In 1854 it was brought to a conclusion. About this time also a version of the New Testament in colloquial Mandarin was carried through the press, for the sake of those who might be more able to understand it in that form. It was Providential that these translations were prosecuted at the time they were actually done. The hand of death was soon after laid upon Dr. Medhurst the veteran and experienced Missionary at the head of the Committee, of which only one member now remains, Mr. Stronach, whose high scholarship gave cast and character to the Delegates' version of the Bible.

No sooner was the work closed than it was resolved by the British and Foreign Bible Society to circulate it far and wide. The late Rev. John Angell James was deeply interested in China, and supposing that the rebellion then going on promised great things in a Christian point of view, he pleaded that a million copies of the New Testament should be printed and circulated. The money was raised for the purpose, and arrangements were made for carrying it into effect. Printing presses were set to work in Shanghai and Hong-kong, and large editions were thrown off for general distribution. At first the missionaries and a few of their converts did what they could in the work, but only in those places and at those distances, which could be reached in the ordinary prosecution of their labours. It was found that this system was inadequate to the wants of the case and the extended opening of the country. Accordingly it was resolved by the Bible Society in 1863, to engage the services of Mr. Alexander Wylie for the special work of superintending the circulation of the Scriptures, as he had been since 1847 in charge of the printing establishment in Shanghai. About the same time, the National Bible Society of Scotland secured the services of the Rev. Alexander Williamson, formerly a Missionary in China, for the same purpose; and at the hands of these two gentlemen, the work of distribution has been carried on to a vast extent. Mr. Wylie has travelled more or less in fourteen of the provinces, having two Europeans, Mr. Johnston and Mr. Welson associated with him as colporteurs. Both of these have done good service in numerous and distant places, and we are grieved to say that the former has apparently lost his life in the course of his labours. He left Shanghai in November 1867, with a view to making his last journey, prior to returning home and studying for the Ministry, as he had it in view to qualify himself for Missionary work in China. He has never been heard of since, and we fear that he was murdered by the way along with his native companions. The Rev. Mr. Williamson has distinguished himself by his travels in Manchuria, Mongolia, and several of the northern provinces. He has trodden new ground in the course of his extensive journeys, and interested many by his intelligent observations in the countries and districts over which he has gone. Hundreds of thousands of copies of the Scriptures have thus been circulated, in parts or in complete volumes, and having been chiefly by sale, there is greater likelihood of their being appreciated by the people, while their meaning and design were explained at the time of distribution. Whatever may be the result of this work, there is no doubt of its having been done in a most efficient manner, in a country too where the printed character even is highly valued, and which has been made what it is in civilization and culture, chiefly by means of the native classics. We have done well to furnish the people with the Sacred Volume that has made us in a great measure what we are as a Christian nation. It is not ours to specify the effect of such labours, only we rejoice to bear witness to the devoted and zealous way in which the operations of the Bible Societies have been carried on in China at the hands of their able representatives.

In addition to this department, much has been done in connexion with the Religious Tract Society. It has nobly seconded our Missionary efforts, and helped us to extend the knowledge of the Gospel by means of a large series of interesting and useful books. Many of these are original, others are modified translations of standard works at home, and suited to the varied requirements of the people. They have been distributed widely, and the whole amounts to many millions of pages. We are in circumstances to be assured of their being extensively read, and of their being of great service in the onward progress of our work. They consist for the most part of commentaries on Scripture, the evidences of Christianity, summaries of Gospel Truth, refutations of idolatry, illustrations of practical religion, and other things.

We are happy in being able to testify to the admirable operations of our American and German brethren in the same field. No distinction is to be drawn between the English Missionaries and them in the matter. We are on a level in every respect, and in the departments we are now referring to as well as in all others, we have laboured together for the evangelization of China. We allude to this simply to convey the idea that all the Missionaries are working for one object, and we wish to be regarded as identified with each other in the prosecution of it. We are thankful for this, and only pray that our union and harmony may be even more complete than it is.

It may be worth while to note that the literary efforts of the Missionary body have been directed to various other objects than those just spoken of. We have thought it useful to enlighten the Chinese mind on matters of science and general knowledge, as being promotive of our great work. Many of the Chinese are capable of appreciating books on such subjects, as have been translated and circu-

L

lated to a considerable extent. We enumerate the following topics—Medicine and Surgery, Mathematics and Astronomy, Geography, Botany, Mechanics, Histories of England and America, International Law, and Natural Philosophy. These works are not to be regarded as of a superficial kind. They enter thoroughly into the various points that are taken up, and are suited to convey clear and positive information in regard to them.

A number of works have also been published by different Missionaries, bearing upon the study of the Chinese language, and forming almost the only means of acquiring a knowledge of it. Dictionaries, grammars, dialogues, lessons, chrestomathies and such like have been issued in connexion with several dialects, and many of them are scholarly in their style, and eminently useful in practical application.

Not a few of the Missionaries have added greatly to our knowledge of the history, literature, and religion of China by the able and excellent books which they have published. Let it suffice to mention the Horæ Sinicæ of Morrison, the State and Prospects of China by Medhurst, the Middle Kingdom by Williams, the Chinese Classics by Legge, Notes on Chinese Literature by Wylie, Religious Condition of the Chinese by Edkins, Social Life of China by Doolittle, and the Medical Missionary by Lockhart. To these might be added many others of greater or less importance, all showing the character and standing of the men connected with the Chinese Missions, and to whom we are indebted for much valuable information about that part of the world.

Whatever may be said as to the literary portion of our Missionary labours, we desire it to be borne in mind that preaching the Gospel is the work to which we have felt ourselves specially called. It is the one thing that has been given us to do, and we have endeavoured to do it as best we could. At the different treaty ports, chapels have been built, where from day to day we are in the habit of proclaiming the Word. The attendance varies from a few to several hundreds at a time, and as occasion offers, we converse with the people or preach to them in the freest and fullest manner.

The method of our discourses, particularly in the case of our best and most experienced Missionaries, is adapted to the circumstances and capacity of the audience. A growing acquaintance is formed with their requirements in this respect, and, speaking generally, the address of St. Paul to the Athenians furnishes an excellent model for us to imitate. Whether intentionally or not, we often proceed on the same ground, as there is a wonderful adaptation in it to the condition of things around us. We are obliged to dwell upon the first principles of natural religion in opposition to their atheism and idolatry, and find the advantage of quoting their native classics, in correspondence with the passage,—" for we are also his offspring." Many parallel sentiments can be adduced, which are well known to our hearers, and which form the occasion of a direct appeal in the matter of their prevailing idolatry and superstition. This leads to the revelation of God's grace, the necessity of repentance, the solemnities of the judgment day, and the verities of the Christian faith—" Jesus and the resurrection."

The reception we meet with in the course of these labours is varied. There are those who hold us and our message in contempt. There are others who treat the subject with indifference and unconcern, while there are some who have had their interest awakened, and their attention directed savingly to eternal things. We are called to meet their difficulties and answer their inquiries. Their main objections arise from the prevailing worship of heaven and earth, their ancestors, their sages, and the idols in the temples. They say that it is hard for them to believe in present circumstances, when their friends and neighbours are all against them. They cannot bear to stand alone, and be exposed to all the inconvenience arising from a change of faith. Persecution and suffering are occasionally threatened. If others would believe, they would do so too, and if the Emperor could only be brought to accept the Christian doctrine, and order all his people in a like manner, the whole nation would soon be converted. The foreign aspect of the system also is an obstacle in their way. They are fearful lest any alteration on their part would be injurious to themselves, their households, or even their departed ancestors. They profess a readiness in some instances to compromise the matter, by an accommodation between their own systems and ours, and "the offence of the cross," the intolerance of Christianity in this respect, is looked upon as strange and unreasonable. There are many also who cannot apprehend the self-denial and spirituality of the Gospel, in its character and requirements. They can perform their idolatrous services in an ordinary, external manner, without interfering with their comfort or advantage, but the claims of our holy religion are peculiar in their view, and form a stumbling-block which is difficult to overcome. So utterly unaccustomed have they been to think of divine things at all, so ignorant and earthly are they in their general habits and sentiments, so stereotyped and formal in their religious life and character, that it is almost impossible to excite in them any thought or feeling on the subject. They presume that the concerns of God, and heaven, and eternity, are infinitely beyond their powers of understanding, and that they have nothing whatever to do with them. Their wisest men gave no information in regard to them, while their priests are at hand to perform the usual ceremonies at death and burial, which may or may not avail, as the case may be. The scepticism and listlessness thus to be encountered, in our endeavours to bring before the Chinese the truths of the Gospel, are such as only the Missionary himself can apprehend; and often is his heart sickened and pained, as he contemplates the peculiarly hardened and stolid condition of the people.

Such more or less is our experience in the chapels, where it is our custom daily to mingle with the heathen, and ascertain their thoughts and sentiments about religious things. The same in measure is found in all our other preaching labours. We do not confine ourselves to stated places and times of worship. In the neighbourhood, there are many populous thoroughfares, where we have splendid opportunities for engaging in our Mission work. In the public tea-gardens, in the area of a heathen temple, in any open and unoccupied ground, near a great concourse of people, we are accustomed to stand up and bear testimony to the Gospel of Christ. In the surrounding country also, among the villages, towns, and cities, we have formed various mission stations, and there, as well as in the streets and other convenient places, we have largely prosecuted our high calling. Beyond these again, in the inland districts and provinces extending over hundreds and thousands of miles, we have made known the Word of Life. Weeks and months have thus been spent by some of our number, and the grandest scope has been enjoyed in the discharge of our blessed work. This has been the case at many different points, and so a vast extent of country has been gone over, north and south, east and west. We attach great importance to this course of itinerant effort. Whatever may be the apparent result of it, or even though there seems to be no results at all, we are persuaded that it is necessary for the general diffusion of the Gospel. Some men are better suited for this line of labour than for anything else, and by all means they ought to fulfil their apostolic ministry in this way. Labours of this kind are found to be a great relief from more local and monotonous work. It gives life and elasticity to a Missionary to go into the interior for a time, and herald to the multitudes around him the message of salvation. The scenery and associations inspire him with fresh zeal, while he is preparing the people for the understanding and ultimate reception of the truth. They cannot be expected to embrace it all at once, but in due time its influence will be felt as the knowledge of it is increasingly imparted. We wish indeed that a well organized system of evangelistic work were established in connexion with the different missions, so as to extend the Gospel into regions where it is seldom or has never been preached. Apart from the spiritual results of it, we are persuaded that if undertaken by judicious and experienced men, it would exert a beneficial effect upon the people at large, in allaying their prejudices, and rendering them amenable to good impressions.

What as to the practical result of our Missionary labours? It is impossible for us to tell the full amount of it. Duty is ours, events are God's. It is a great thing to be able to preach the Gospel, so widely and so freely in many parts of China. It has not been the case for any great length of time, and we have had much preparatory work to do in acquiring the language, in familiarizing the people with us, in breaking up the fallow or rather the stony ground, and in sowing the seed of Divine truth "beside all waters." But what are the statistics of our Mission field? The *Missionary Journal* of July 1869, gives full details on the subject, and it appears from it that the number of persons in full communion with the different churches existing in China, amounted at that time to upwards of five thousand seven hundred. These have raised during the past year, above four thousand dollars for various purposes in connexion with them. Wherever the Missions have been engaged a sufficient length of time, they have not failed in reaping a certain measure of success. Twenty years ago there were hardly twenty converts belonging to the Protestant Missions in the country, and the above shows what advance has been made since then. It is to be expected that our success will go on in an increasing ratio, corresponding, under God, to the work that is done, and the efficiency of the men engaged in it.

Are we asked what is the character and standing of the converts thus made? Our answer is that this ought to be considered in connexion with the circumstances of the case. Their past history, and the influences brought to bear upon them in their natural heathen state must not be forgotten. Even then, however, we are free to confess the grace of God evidently at work in the hearts and lives of many of our Christian converts. The great majority are of the lower or humbler classes of society, who were formerly given to idolatry and superstition. They have now been reclaimed from these, and profess faith in Christ as the only ground of acceptance with God. Others were the devoted followers of Confucius, and the venerated sages of their country. They were imbued with the pride and prejudice, the atheism and materialism characteristic of such men, but they now acknowledge the Lord Jesus, and worship the only true and living God. We have often reason, it is true, for anxiety and sorrow on account of some connected with us, and have occasion for the exercise of severe discipline on their account. But this is not surprising, when we consider their position and early training. It obtained to no small extent in the primitive church, and is to be found among ourselves at home. At the same time we are satisfied that the work of sanctification in the Bible sense of it has been commenced, and is going on in the experience and conduct of many of our Chinese Christians. We do not boast beyond our measure in this line of things, but we sincerely bless God for what has been done. There are numbers in our churches whom we would not hesitate to place on a level with our approved fellow Christians at home. Their knowledge of divine truth, their earnestness and intelligence in prayer, their firm attachment to the Gospel in spite of the evils and errors around them, their diligent observance of the means of grace, their hearty and entire renunciation of idolatry, and their endeavours to bring their heathen countrymen to repent and believe in Christ, are grounds of great encouragement to us in our Missionary work. There are not a few among them, who have shown a high degree of qualification as native teachers, and preachers, and pastors, who have been appointed to such positions in the church, and who have given us much satisfaction from their piety, their ability, their excellent moral character, and their usefulness in various fields of labour. Many instances of this kind might be adduced in connexion with our different Missions. Each Missionary has his own reason for thankfulness in the matter, and looks upon his native brethren in the ministry as of invaluable service to him. There is no doubt a striking contrast between the foreign Missionary and his native assistants in their national character and habits. The one is strong, impulsive, bold and aggressive in his manner and bearing, ever suggesting new and onward modes of operation, marked and followed more fully by the natives, though it may be from curiosity, and is believed in by them as thoroughly sincere in his profession and practice. The others are more timid and cautious, limited in their sphere of action, yet able to come into closer contact with the people, to excite their confidence, and to prepare them for the better understanding and open acceptance of the Gospel. The two are in fact indispensable to each other, and may profit largely from mutual counsel and assistance. The time is evidently coming on when the churches already formed must be left more in native hands, allowing the foreign Missionary to extend the Gospel into other parts, and to exercise only a general supervision of the Missions that have been established. Still the Missions in China are in their infancy. We must not precipitate new measures, though there may be as great danger in keeping the converts in a dependent state, and relying too much and too long upon foreign aid and oversight. As it is, we see in these churches the fruit of our Missionary toil, and as we contemplate them, we thank God and take courage.

We cannot close this chapter without referring to other departments of labour, that have an important bearing upon our great object. From an early period in the history of Protestant Missions in China, medical men have been engaged in connexion with them. We have witnessed the operation of these medical Missions with extreme interest. They have been the means of doing immense good, both in alleviating human misery, and in furnishing opportunity for preaching the Gospel. In Canton, Swatow, Amoy, Ningpo, Shanghai, Hankow, and Pekin, such institutions have been at work for a number of years, and they have been largely availed of by the Chinese. Though strongly attached to their own native systems, many are not in circumstances to make use of them, while they are found to be inefficient in a great variety of cases. There can be no doubt as to the salutary effect of our foreign treatment in myriads of instances; and it is an excellent way of testifying to the benevolent spirit of our Christianity. It is appreciated in this point of view as much as the Chinese are capable of doing so. But they are not left to learn the fact merely from what they see and feel. These institutions are directly the means of instructing the people in Divine things. Missionaries—native and foreign —are in the habit of holding religious service about the time of attending the patients, when books are distributed and the word is preached to them. This is a recognized element of every day's work; and so multitudes are led to hear the Gospel, who might never hear it otherwise. Many of them come from distant and different parts of the country, and have it in their power to carry the knowledge of mercy thither, along with the report of the benefit conferred upon them, by means of the foreign medicine. Not a few instances of spiritual and saving good have occurred as a result of these conjoint labours; and it is to be hoped that the work will be continued and extended as much as possible. In the opening of new Missions, the system is of great advantage; but it requires much life and interest to be thrown into it, to prevent its becoming an ordinary and monotonous thing, and the moral benefit of it being merged in the material. We give all honour to the men engaged in this capacity. There is so much of self-denial in medicating for the Chinese, that it cannot be for the mere pleasure of it that the work is carried on. Their annual reports are deeply interesting in a medical point of view, and are the means of communicating valuable information, which does not fall within the usual province of a Missionary.

Various Missions have prosecuted school teaching with great advantage. The number on the list in all parts is 4,500 boys and girls. This is the place for saying a few words on the subject. Education is highly valued and extensively pursued in China. Schools and seminaries are everywhere to be found, but they are for boys only, while the girls are neglected, and very few of them are able to read at all. There are several reasons for this, not in the way of depreciating its usefulness even to them; but there is no apprehension of its necessity in their case. It it thought that the girls will have no occasion for reading and writing, and that they will be married into other families, who will have the enjoyment and benefit of them, without the trouble and expense of their education. Besides, as it is no easy matter to proceed in a course of Chinese study, it is not thought worth while for the girls to practice it in the laborious orthodox form. They are kept at home, therefore, helping in the various duties of the family, until the time comes when they shall be removed to another circle. All that is wanted at their hands, when they grow up is, that they shall be able to attend to the ordinary departments of female life, such as washing, embroidery, or weaving, while the art of reading and writing can be dispensed with. As to the boys, many of them go to school for a longer or a shorter time; but the process of learning is in their case too, very tedious, while the information communicated is extremely imperfect. On this account, and from the desirability of imbuing the youthful mind with right and useful knowledge on secular and on religious subjects, some of the Missions have established day and boarding schools, that have been in operation for a series of years. A number of both sexes have in this way been led to join the church, and are giving evidence of the value and benefit of the education they have received. Several of the young men are actively engaged in Missionary work, and have been ordained to the office of the Christian Ministry, with much credit to themselves and advantage to the cause.

Female teaching may be here referred to. Honoured names might be mentioned in this department, illustrating the great importance and usefulness of this kind of labour. We are of the impression that idolatry and superstition are kept up in China mainly through the influence of the women. The mothers teach their children at home and in the temples various acts of religious worship; and so the system is perpetuated from age to age. Were the women only converted, we believe that idolatry would soon cease out of the land. Now they are to be reached specially through their own sex, alike native and foreign, and we cannot too earnestly counsel the employment of such a class of persons in connexion with Missionary work in China. Females—married and unmarried—are capable of doing much useful service in this way; and the latter, in particular, from their being in circumstances to give themselves wholly to it. We strongly recommend the adoption or extension of this kind of effort.

Printing establishments have been formed in connexion with two or three of the Missions, and a vast amount of work has been carried through the press in Chinese and English, and even in Japanese. They have been most serviceable in supplying the various Missions with Bibles, tracts, and other books; and we should have been far less favourably situated had this agency not been employed.

Such is our Missionary work in China. It has somewhat different aspects in different parts of the field, but in the main it is the same everywhere. One district may have more attractions than another, from physical or psychological causes, in the contour of the country, or the character of the people. But the Chinese are one, and require to be preached to in a like manner in all places. They have the same objections against Christianity, and they are in the same moral and spiritual circumstances throughout. We are fully alive to the difficulties of our work. We feel them in their intensest and most aggravated forms, but we are not discouraged. It is a solemn duty in which we are called to engage; and we are sustained and cheered in the prosecution of it by the measure of success we have actually enjoyed. It is all of God, and whether our success be large or small, we are at the best "unprofitable servants." "The treasure is in earthen vessels, that the excellency of the power may be seen to be of God, and not of us." "Not unto us, O Lord, not unto us, but unto Thy name give glory."

CHAPTER VII.

PERSONAL INCIDENT AND ADVENTURE.

On arriving in Shanghai in August, 1847, after a voyage of 133 days, everything appeared strange and novel. There were few foreigners residing there at that time, but the numbers of Chinese, their appearance, dress and manners, struck us with surprise. We had been interested in catching the first sight of the Chinese junks at sea, or at the mouth of the Yang-tsze-kiang, on our way to our destined haven, but the general appearance of Shanghai showed it to be a place of great importance. The country all around was flat. There was nothing of elevation except the numerous graves, that were visible on every side. Shortly before leaving England, we were charged to have our house built on high ground, but it did not seem likely that such would be the case, at all events in this part of the country.

We were kindly received by our predecessors in the Mission, Dr. Medhurst and Mr. Lockhart, and in due time placed in our respective quarters. They had been in Shanghai for four years, and were the pioneers of Protestant Missionary labour in North China. In my early longings to be engaged in the service of Christ among the heathen, I had read Medhurst's State and Prospects of China with deep interest, and had gazed intently upon his likeness in the frontispiece of the book, with the impression on my mind that he was too distinguished a man for me to be associated with in the Mission field. Never did I expect to have such a privilege conferred upon me. But so it was, and I take this opportunity of testifying to my esteem and reverence for his memory. His manner and bearing in the Mission were of the kindliest character, while his devotedness to the work and his manifold labours in connexion with it, formed a noble example to us, that we should be likeminded and follow his steps, when called, however unworthy, to succeed him.

The first thing to be done was the study of the language, and it was undertaken at once as a matter of course. I am not aware that the idea of difficulty ever occurred to me in regard to it. The Chinese teacher was daily at my side, and I prosecuted the work in the way pointed out in the second chapter. Very gradual progress was made, but in time I found that I could communicate a few ideas to my preceptor, and I was encouraged in my earnest desires to go among the people and speak to them, though in stammering words, about God and Christ. Accompanied by my teacher, I went to some of the principal thoroughfares in the city with a number of tracts in my hand, and the sight of a foreigner standing up in these circumstances soon drew a large crowd around me. The result generally was that I broke down, but I succeeded in leading many to the neighbouring chapel where Dr. Medhurst was preaching, and where they had the opportunity of hearing an excellent sermon. On the Sabbath days, I frequently went to chapel for the purpose of listening to a Chinese discourse, or to the country villages and hamlets along with a native assistant, to distribute Christian books, and tell the people about the way of salvation. These were seasons of high enjoyment. I found myself gaining aptitude in the language, and was emboldened to use it as much as possible. However imperfect my attempts were for a long time, I am satisfied they did myself good, both in improving my linguistic skill, and keeping alive my Missionary zeal, apart from any advantage they did to the people.

My teacher proved to be an inveterate opium smoker, and I was obliged to part with him. Some time afterwards, I visited his native place twenty miles distant, on a Missionary tour, and on making inquiries about him, was informed that his mother had been so indignant at his opium propensities, that she shut him up in a room, where he died from the withholdment of the pipe. If it were so, nothing would be done to her in the circumstances, as she had a right to punish a disobedient son even in this extreme manner, and the occasion of his death was then looked upon as induced by himself.

We were in the habit of prosecuting itinerant work in the country, going and returning in twenty-four hours, according to the arrangement of the Consul. In 1848, Dr. Medhurst, Mr. Lockhart, and myself went to the city of Tsing-pu, thirty miles from Shanghai. We carried on our work as usual, distributing tracts and preaching to the people. At the time there was a number of junks in the stream. They had been employed in conveying the tribute grain of the South to Pekin by the Imperial Canal. It had been resolved, however, to engage sea-going junks that year for the purpose, and the ordinary class of sailors were thus thrown idle. Many of them were at this place. On leaving it, we walked to our boat, which was at the distance of five miles. When not far from the city, we heard loud noises behind us, and looking round observed a number of men coming in our direction armed with clubs, chains, and other instruments. We quickened our pace, but were overtaken and savagely beaten and robbed by our assailants. We sought to reason with them, but in vain, until it seemed to them that we were entirely in their power. They then took hold of us and drove us back towards the city. On passing the gates, as they were proceeding with us to their junks, a large body of Mandarin followers came out and rescued us. We were conducted to the office of the magistrate and kindly treated. We had been sorely bruised, and were scarcely able to walk. A full report of the case was taken down. Our boat was brought close to the city walls, and in due time we left the place. One of the boatmen hearing of our misfortune had gone to Shanghai, where an expedition was being fitted out to come to our help. The matter was thoroughly gone into by the Consul, Mr. (now Sir) Rutherford Alcock. The grain junks were blockaded in the port until redress was obtained. The leading offenders were secured and exposed in the cangue, or pillory, on which their offence was inscribed for the warning of all.

At another time a brother missionary and myself arranged to go into the interior to a considerable distance. It could not be done in our foreign dress, as we should at once have been known and sent back, if not worse treated. Besides, the people were then in a great excitement from the incursions of the rebels, and this increased the difficulty of inland travel. We determined therefore to assume the Chinese dress, with the long tail in addition. The change was effected over night, and we proceeded to our boat. We kept as closely to it as possible, desirous of arriving at the end of our journey, before meeting with any reverse. The country was beautiful, and the limpid streams formed a great attraction to the eye. We passed the city of Suchow, about which the Chinese are fond of saying, *Shang yeu Tien tang, Hia yeu Su Hang*,—that is, above there is heaven and below are Suchow and Hangchow. We resolved to visit this terrestial paradise on our return, and pushed on to Wusih. We went ashore and were recognised by a number of persons, who had often seen Romish Missionaries there in native dress, and no doubt observed the awkwardness of our manners in spite of our disguise. However, we suffered no ill-treatment at their hands, though there were the usual epithets of barbarian and white devil applied to us on every side. We distributed a few books and sailed to Chang-chow about thirty miles distant. Soldiers were in all directions, owing to the rebels who were at Chinkiang some sixty miles off. We cast anchor and were visited by a number of small officials. At length one of higher standing came on board with fear and trembling, scarcely venturing to trust himself near us. We told him who we were and desired him not to be afraid. He then entered on the troubled state of the country, and entreated that on going back to Shanghai, we should endeavour to prevail on the Consul to send a steamer to Chinkiang, as he believed such a vessel had mighty power and could do great wonders. If this were done, he said, and the rebels were driven away, we could engage in commerce to a large extent, and especially in rhubarb, which he thought foreigners highly valued.

Ere long we left the place to return home, and

on arriving at Suchow we landed. Books were distributed and the word was preached. We were returning to our boat when one of us was laid hold of. On endeavouring to get away, the hue and cry was raised, and a multitude was soon gathered round. We were seized by our tails and driven back to the city. The crowd increased until a vast array of human heads was seen in all directions. Many were now laying hold of our caudal appendages, and they tugged mine so furiously that I thought they would soon pull my head off altogether. My companion was in better circumstances than I was, from having less hair of his own, or from his tail not being so strongly attached to it, and so the two happily parted company after a short time. I wished with all my heart that mine would do so too, but in spite of the numbers that were dragging and pulling at it the tail remained. On the way a man came out of a coffin shop, and gave me a heavy blow on the head with a lump of wood, when I began to abandon all hope, resigning myself into the hands of Him, whose I was and whom I served. We were taken to a police station at the side of the road, and questioned at all hands as to whom we were. Our replies were explicit enough, that we were foreigners from Shanghai, and were religious teachers engaged in exhorting the people to do good. They insisted upon our being rebels, and asked if we were not aware that a price was offered for our heads. We sought permission to go into a neighbouring tea-shop which was granted, and while there, a body of officers from the magistracy came and took us through the immense crowd filling the streets. On arriving at the office of the district magistrate, we were subjected for several hours to a rigid examination, and asked all manner of questions about Shanghai, to ascertain if we were really true men and no spies. Meanwhile our boatmen were being similarly examined, and at the end it was agreed by the magistrates that we were no doubt what we professed to be. They came to us and said, "We believe you to be foreigners, very good men indeed, but you know you had no right to come into this city. Your only proper place is the treaty port of Shanghai. We have interfered for your deliverance this time, but we shall not do it again if you dare to come here any more. At present the people are in a state of great confusion. We shall endeavour to quiet them, and you must remain until night, when we hope it will be safe to take you back to your boat. Remember, however, you are never to be seen in Suchow again." We thanked them for their kindness without promising to do what they wanted. We were duly conveyed to our boat, and sailed to Shanghai. A day or two after, I went to the Mission chapel in the city, and the first man that entered was from Suchow. I asked him if any trouble had occurred there a few days previously. He said they had caught two rebels. What was done to them? They were taken to the office of the district magistrate, and next morning a declaration was posted up to the effect that they had been privately beheaded. I told him that I happened to be one of them, and of course he looked at me with great astonishment.

On numerous occasions have we met with treatment of a trying and hazardous kind, in the course of our itinerant labours, from a number of ill-disposed persons mingling in the crowd usually following us. In addition to the ordinary disparaging epithets, we have often heard the savage and brutal yell, "beat and kill the barbarian." Brickbats, stones, and other missiles have been wildly thrown at us and our boats, rendering it unsafe to travel in such districts, though on the other hand vast tracts of country have been gone over, without any serious injury or harm. In either case, we trust that God has given us grace to say,—"none of these things move us, neither count we our lives dear unto us, that we may finish our course with joy, and the ministry we have received of the Lord Jesus."

I was once sailing outside the Wusung river, with several native assistants, when a cry was raised by the boatmen, "*Kiang-taou, kiang-taou,*" pirates, pirates. I went on deck and saw a large boat bearing down close upon us, with a number of men on board armed with boathooks to lay hold of our vessel. When they saw me they consulted together, and happily turned off in a different direction. We were near the entrance of an inland stream, and on getting into it, the natives who had observed the piratical craft, congratulated us on our safety, as they expected to have seen us attacked and plundered.

Our mode of travelling in the neighbourhood of Shanghai is chiefly by means of boats. The canals and streams are abundant, and run a long way into the interior. We can proceed in this manner for days and weeks at a time. The boats are very comfortable, and supplies of food are easily obtained on the way. In sailing along, we pass numerous villages, towns, and cities, and on leaving the boat at the side of the stream, we walk ashore amongst the people, distributing our books in the shops, and giving them to persons whom we meet. At various distances, we stand up on the side of the road or in some public place, and preach to as many as may assemble. We continue doing so from morning to night, and with little interval, and are able in this way to accomplish a great amount of work, going from end to end of large and populous cities, and making known the Gospel to thousands in the course of the day. We do not always labour together, but pass and repass each other in a continuous line for several hours, uniting only on coming into the area of a heathen temple, which may form a suitable gathering place for a crowd of people. During these labours, inquiries are answered and objections met, as we endeavour to make the preaching as conversational as possible, and only for a short time at each place, unless it is attended with special interest. We are thus able to go over a vast extent of ground, and gratifying instances have occurred in which it has been found that we have not preached the Word in vain. These itinerant efforts have always afforded us much pleasure and satisfaction, being assured that we were thus sowing the seed of Divine truth, and making the Gospel known to many who would not otherwise have heard it. About a month after preaching in a new field in this manner, a brother Missionary inquired if I knew of any one that had been labouring there. I told him that I did, and on asking the reason of his inquiry, he said, that his Mission had established a book-store at a considerable distance from it in another province. One day a native came into the store, and stated that a foreigner had been preaching in his city about God and Jesus. He had heard him, and learning that it was possible to obtain books on the subject in that place, he had come to purchase them. He bought about half-a-crown's worth, and was much pleased with being able to do so. Various cases might be narrated of spiritual good following these evangelistic labours, which have been so largely prosecuted in the country.

In 1858, we heard that a change had taken place in the outflow of the Yellow River. We could not get any information about it in Shanghai. All that the natives were able to say of it was, that the river "*puh tsai kia le*," that is, it was not at home. We have already mentioned that this river has been often the occasion of much trouble to China, from its breaking through its embankments, and deluging the surrounding country, till it found a new outlet for its waters to the sea. The bed of the river was really higher than the neighbouring fields, and so the banks required to be carefully attended to like the dykes of Holland. The Mandarins, however, are not over honest in this matter, or in anything else; though drawing the needful supplies from government, they often peculate a considerable amount, and neglect the requirements of the work. In this case, the inevitable consequences had happened. The river when in flood had broken through a weak place of the embankments, and gone in a new direction. It was on this account that numbers of the men ordinarily engaged in this department had been thrown out of employment, and these have now for a long time taken to marauding and plunder. Several provinces are in a state of chronic rebellion from this cause, and untold misery has fallen upon the people in consequence. But what as to the river? Two of us resolved to make a Missionary tour in that direction. We left Shanghai, reached the northern parts of Kiang-nan, crossed the Yang-tsze, entered into new territory, and commenced our work of preaching in the towns and villages along the Grand Canal. Our journey was intensely interesting from the novelty of it, and the opportunity it gave us of proclaiming the Gospel in these unknown districts. As a whole, the people seemed inferior in cultivation to those whom we had left behind, and the country was much poorer. We pushed on our way, and at length arrived at Tsinkiang-pu, the end we had proposed to ourselves. It appeared to be a large and populous place, distant from Shanghai about 450 miles. No sooner was it noised abroad that foreigners had come thither, than the people assembled in great numbers. The sides of the Canal were crowded, and on casting anchor, Mandarins of various grades came on board to ask who we were, and what was our object. We told them that we were *muh-sze*, ministers or pastors, but they had no idea of this religious designation, and that having heard that the Yellow River had disappeared, we were anxious to see if it was the case. They said it was a long way off, and that it was impossible for us to get near to it. The day was hot, and we resolved to remain quietly in our boats till the afternoon. About four o'clock we hastily stepped ashore, to the astonishment of those on board, and no less of the multitudes on the banks, whose crowded lines we went through, and proceeding in the right direction, we soon reached the former bed of the river. It was as dry as dust, and we had the satisfaction of preaching upon it to those who followed us, after which we crossed to the other side, and walked along the banks, observing the deep valley below which had been not long before the bed of one of the greatest rivers in the world. Next morning we went a considerable distance, and noticed the locks through which the grain-carrying junks had been accustomed to go, on their voyage from the Central to the Northern parts of the empire. An old temple was at the side, in which was an idol under whose protection the Canal had been placed, and to which the sailors had long been in the habit of paying respect, that they might be prospered in their voyage. It was through this that the embassy of Lord Amherst went in 1816 to Pekin, and the circumstances of it compared with our own at the time, rendered the sights and scenes around most interesting.

In 1866, I went to the North of China, calling at Chefoo and Newchwang on the way to Tientsin and Pekin. A few days before arriving at the former place, a vessel had sailed from it to Corea, on board of which was the Rev. Mr. Thomas, my former fellow-labourer in the Mission at Shanghai, who was then connected with the Mission at Pekin. He was a remarkable linguist, and devoted to travelling greatly for the purpose of adding to his stock of languages. He never returned, and it is believed that he and all on board were murdered by the Coreans. The particulars have not been fully ascertained.

On getting to Newchwang, we were gratified from its being on new ground, different from what we had been accustomed to for nearly twenty years. It is in Manchuria. I went round the native city, preached in various directions, and was much pleased with the aspect of the place. There seemed to be a population of about 40,000, and as there was no Missionary amongst them, I hoped the field would soon be occupied. Not long after, the Rev. Wm. C. Burns, of the English Presbyterian Mission, went there, and laboured for a time in an infirm state of health. He persevered to the end, and died from sheer exhaustion. He was a noble and devoted man, eminently pious, and had done good service by his evangelistic life and labours at home and abroad. He was esteemed, honoured, and loved by his Missionary brethren of all denominations. We are glad to know that Newchwang is now occupied by Missionaries of the Irish Presbyterian Mission, and it is our prayer that God may bless them in their work.

A few days after reaching Tientsin, we left for the Capital, the very sight of which was deeply impressive to a stranger. There were many objects of interest and curiosity to be seen in it, but the celebrated Temple of Heaven exceeded them all in our estimation. We were indebted to the kindness of Dr. Dudgeon for the way in which he succeeded in getting us within the walls. The history and design of the place were in our view most sacred, and one could only think of the Temple of Solomon in connexion with it.

It was arranged by the Rev. Mr. Edkins that we should take a journey into Mongolia, in order to fix upon a place for the establishment of a Mongolian Mission. The London Missionary Society had a Mission formerly in that region, under the Rev. Messrs. Swan and Stallybrass, which had been discontinued by the command of the late Emperor Nicholas of Russia. It had been reported to Mr. Edkins, that a number of Mongols had abandoned their nomadic life, and settled down at a town called Kwei-Hwa. It seemed that this would prove a likely spot for the proposed Mission. We left Pekin, and enjoyed the journey in the highest degree. The Great Wall of China through which we passed, was peculiarly interesting. The appearance of the towns and villages presented a striking contrast to similar places in the South. Occasionally we came across settlements consisting of excavations on the side of a hill, and which called to mind what we had heard in our early study of the Chinese classics, regarding the primitive mode of living among the first settlers in the country. This is always spoken of by the teachers with great respect and veneration. In four or five days we arrived at Kalgan, where we were kindly received by Mr. and Mrs. Gulicke, of the American Board of Foreign Missions. They had been labouring there for some time. The place was thoroughly Chinese, with a sprinkling of Mongols to be seen here and there, but mostly as coming from the country, on camels or horses. They were looked upon by us with much interest, from the object we had in view. In due time arrangements were made for the prosecution of our journey, and carts were secured for the purpose. These are the chief means of conveyance in the North, from the absence of large streams. We went through the high gates of the city, and at once touched on Mongolian ground. Our first steps were for hours up a steep ravine, which forms the bed of a river in rainy weather. About four o'clock in the afternoon we reached the top, when we found ourselves on a level with the heights around. It was an extended grassy plain, altogether new country to us. We proceeded to a Mongol encampment, where we were hospitably entertained. The inhabitants were different in many respects from the Chinese, whom they disliked, while they seemed to be very favourably disposed to us, as we had never made such attacks upon them, and their ancestral property, as the Chinese have done. We had much interesting conversation with them, Mr. Edkins chiefly in the Mongolian tongue, and I in Chinese, which most of them could readily understand. They were devoted Buddhists, and presented a remarkable contrast in the simplicity and earnestness of their faith to the scepticism and indifference of their Chinese neighbours.

Our journey for several days was rather monotonous from the scenery around us, except when we came across a cultivated part of the country, which struck us with surprise, and was found to be owing to the industry of the Chinese settled there. It stood out in remarkable contrast to the indolent or nomadic habits of the Mongols. On one occasion, we were passing a beautiful temple which we went to see. It was formed after the Thibetan model, and was a pleasing specimen of that architecture. On talking with the priests about the place, we asked if we could see their head Lama. We were told that we could, and were taken to a small room where was a youth of thirteen years of age. He was well dressed, and we were informed that he was their *Guggen*, or holy one, a term corresponding in part to a living Buddha. He was very timid in regard to us, never having seen foreigners before. We presented him with a copy of Swan's Mongolian Testament. Shortly after he asked those around him if it was time to go, when they took him in their arms and carried him outside. He was placed on horseback, and on inquiring if we could follow him, it was readily consented to. We walked for a quarter of a mile and arrived at a neat looking temple into which the youth had been taken. He was placed on a table or altar, at the foot of a large image of Buddha, and in a crosslegged manner, similar to that of the image,—the form in which Buddha is always represented when engaged in contemplation or instructing his disciples. There were about twenty priests in the room, who commenced a religious service in the way of chanting Mongolian or Thibetan hymns in honour of Buddha. The youth was occupied in the same way, though his attention was greatly directed to the strangers. In the front verandah, there was a number of persons bowing down very reverently towards the youth and the image behind him. On coming away, I asked a priest whom these persons were worshipping—the image or the *Guggen?* His answer was, they are one and the same, as the Buddha, represented by the image, actually lives in the breast of the *Guggen*. As such he was the object of their reverent worship and had been so for some years. The idea is that the spirit of old Buddha is always reproduced on earth. When a Grand Lama dies, whose residence is in Lassa, the capital of Thibet, he is succeeded by a child into whom his spirit is supposed to have entered; and it has been politically arranged by the Chinese Government that the leading banners or tribes of Mongols should be presided over by a corresponding number of the Buddhist hierarchy, or it may be one of the second order, for the sake of preserving them in peace, and preventing a national rising on their part. Our idea is in harmony with the system of transmigration, that the youth may have been supposed to have attained a wonderful degree of merit in a former state, so that when born in this life he had reached the *Guggenship*, and in a future birth he may attain to the rank of a Buddha, of whom, as the classics say, there may be " as many as there are sands on the Ganges."

We arrived at the termination of our journey and found the city occupied by Chinese and only a few Mongols. There were temples of the latter kind in various parts, having as many as 1000 or 2000 priests connected with them. They are engaged in travelling about the country among the tribes that are scattered there. The conclusion to which we came was, that judging from what we had seen and the difficulty of visiting all parts of the country, as well as the uncertainty of meeting large numbers of Mongols, except at markets and like places, it would be better to establish the Missionary at Pekin itself. In the winter time, thousands of Mongols repair thither to sell their game and receive their annual allowance from Government as soldiers liable to conscription in the army. These come from all quarters, and most useful service can be done amongst them. We are glad to know that a Missionary has been appointed for this purpose, and so the work necessarily abandoned many years ago, will be resumed in a new sphere and under more favourable auspices.

In the seventeenth century, a colony of Jews

was discovered in Kai-fung-foo, the capital of Honan, on the banks of the Yellow River. They seemed at that time to be in a poor condition, and their synagogue was in a dilapidated state. Nothing more was heard of them for about 200 years. In 1853, Miss Cook of London, wrote Bishop Smith of Hong Kong, to make inquiries about them. He applied to Dr. Medhurst, and two of the converts were sent to Kai-fung, about 600 miles distant. They returned after a time with two of the Jews, having a number of Hebrew manuscripts, consisting of the Pentateuch and prayers, copies of various inscriptions, and a plan of the temple. The appearance of the former was thoroughly Chinese, but they declared most strongly their national antecedents. We ascertained that the colony had been established in China from the beginning of the Christian era, or even prior to it. For at least fifty years they had lost the knowledge of the Hebrew letters, and they seemed glad of their recognition by us. They returned home in two or three weeks, not without bearing sad proofs of their opium smoking propensities, in which way they largely spent their money that had been given them for their valuable manuscripts. Some of these indicated their connexion with Persian Jews about three centuries before. We did not hear of them for a long time afterwards. The country being open from Pekin, however, they have been visited since, and the last news is that their synagogue has disappeared, having been taken down by some of their number and the materials sold to the heathen. The others were exasperated at it probably from their not having shared in the spoil, and now the only remaining monument of the Jewish faith on the ground so long occupied by their temple are two stone tablets describing their origin and entrance into China, of which we got a copy at the hands of our two messengers. The Jews now bear the name of the *Tiaou-kin-kiaou,* or the pluck-sinew-religion, in allusion to the incident in Jacob's life when he wrestled with the angel. They gave themselves this name at the time of the Romish persecution, fearing they would be identified with the Catholics, and suffer accordingly. They are now greatly reduced in number and circumstances. Probably there are two hundred families in all. Some of them profess a desire to receive instruction at our hands, and have sent several of their children to Pekin for this object.

On one occasion I was preaching in our Mission Chapel, and when I closed, a middle-aged man stood up and addressed the people in an earnest manner. He seemed to do it very properly, and when he concluded, I asked who he was, and if he had ever heard this doctrine before? He told me that he had never done so. Why then do you speak in this way? I am persuaded, he said, that it is true, and am compelled to speak accordingly.

I desired him to come again, which he promised to do. He repeated his visits to the chapel, and in course of time we were well satisfied with him, so that he was baptized and received into the church. He seemed an apt and ready speaker, and was made use of in preaching to his countrymen, both in the city and at a distance. The story that he subsequently gave of his conversion was to the following effect. He was going into the tea-gardens with a friend, but happened to see the chapel doors open. He came inside and heard the preacher, who spoke of all men being sinners and liable to punishment, when he said to himself " I knew all this before; I have done many things wrong and deserve to go to hell for it, but to have come here merely to hear this, was of no use." The next thing the Missionary spoke about was the idols, as worthless and unable to benefit the worshipper in anywise. Our friend thought that he was well aware of this too. He had often worshipped the idols in the temple, but had obtained no good from it, so he considered it of little use to come into the chapel and listen merely to this. The preacher then proceeded to enlarge upon works of merit, when the same sentiment was expressed, and the same impression produced. Finally, it was asked, since man was in such a sinful, helpless, and hopeless condition, what was to be done? In reply, the fact was announced that Jesus Christ had come from heaven to atone for human sin and give to all eternal life.

The views deeply affected our friend. He had never heard the like of it before. He accepted the Gospel then and there, and believed that he would have done it previously had he enjoyed the opportunity of hearing it. He continued in the faith of it to his dying day, when he sent a message to the writer that he was still trusting in Jesus, and hoped to meet him in the better world.

A Chinese scholar came from the city of Suchow. He had distinguished himself at the native examinations. He had heard of the Gospel, and came to Shanghai partly with a view to become better acquainted with it. He was placed over a Chinese school, belonging to the Mission. Christian books were placed in his hands, and he attended the services in the chapel. Gradually light dawned upon his mind. He professed himself a follower of Christ, and was baptized. His family came into the neighbourhood. His eldest son was about twelve years of age, who, after a time, showed such pleasing indications of religious knowledge and piety, that he also was baptized, as well as the other members of his family. The son became very ill. I went to see him. It was evident he could not live long. The father entered the room with me, crying bitterly at the thought of the early death of his eldest boy. His son said, "Father, do not weep, I believe in Jesus, and am very happy." In a short time he said again, "Father, I want you to meet me in heaven." He uttered these words three times in an impressive and solemn tone. Not long after this he died. Years passed on, and the father showed himself to be a most consistent follower of Christ, and highly qualified for the sacred office of the ministry. His ordination was resolved on, and as it was proceeding, he was asked as to his faith in Christ, and his reasons for desiring the office to which he was being appointed. His reply, in the presence of several hundreds of his countrymen, was as follows: "It is true that I professed to believe in Jesus, prior to the death of my eldest son, but it was not until he said to me in solemn and emphatic terms, 'Father, I want you to meet me in heaven;' that the thing went to my heart, and from that time I gave myself, body, soul, and spirit, to be the Lord's. Now I desire to live and die in His service, and when called away, I hope to go and see my dear boy again in heaven." He is still living, adorning his Christian profession, and regarded with the highest esteem by all his fellow-disciples.

The first baptisms which I performed in China were in the case of two of my scholars. They were about seventeen or eighteen years of age. They had been in the school for several years. Several of my Missionary brethren examined them and were much pleased with them. They were baptized in the presence of a large congregation. One of them lived for five or six years, and was engaged at last as a Bible colporteur. He was taken ill of cholera. I visited him, and as his case seemed hopeless, I asked him if he was afraid to die. He said, "Oh, no, teacher, I believe in Jesus Christ, and trust in Him, whatever happens to me." I told him that it was feared he would not live long; had he anything to say to his mother about his burial? She was not a Christian. He called her and said, "Mother, you know that I have professed to be a follower of Jesus. I wish you to believe in Him too; and I beg that you will not call the heathen priests to perform any of their religious ceremonies at my death." We have reason to believe that the promise was kept, which is not always the case in regard to the converts, as their friends often interfere and insist upon the observance of the usual rites on the occasion. The other youth is still living and doing good and excellent service in the Chinese hospital. He has been there for nearly fifteen years, and is a humble-minded, consistent Christian. Would that we could tell the same story, in reference to all the other boys who were under training in our Mission school. Like our fellow-labourers in the field, we have had our trials and disappointments in many ways; but we are cheered by any tokens of success graciously bestowed upon us, and are thankful that the work is not more discouraging than it is.

One of our first converts was a remarkable man. He had been a chief disciple of a reformer in the country, who opposed some of the doctrines of the celebrated commentator on the Chinese classics. He had numerous followers. This man came to Shanghai in the prosecution of his business. He was a tea merchant, and was brought under the sound of the Gospel. He became impressed with what he heard, and asked if it was really true. The Missionary dilated upon the miracles of Christ. He listened attentively, and at the end said, "that the Buddhist priests profess to do such things also, but they were not believed." The Missionary then spoke of his own experience, adopting the moral argument of Christianity. He referred to his own convictions of sin, and his fear of the consequences, till he came to the knowledge and acceptance of the Gospel. The man was rivetted. Tears were observed running down his cheeks, and he said, "if such was the spiritual power of the Gospel, I desire to believe it and become a follower of Jesus Christ." Often have I been struck with the gravity and solemnity of this early convert to the faith. He endeavoured to bring the Missionary into contact with his reforming teacher, going with him into the interior at the time when it was dangerous to do so, and hoping that a coalescence might take place between the two. The reformer, however, sent word that he was unwell, and that it was inconvenient to have the meeting that was proposed. Thus it was in China as it was in early days. Gallio and Seneca seemed both to have had the opportunity of conversing with Paul, but "they cared for none of these things," whatever may have been their moral character and teaching in other respects.

I was much interested one day by the seventy-fifth descendant of the sage Confucius calling upon me. His name and title was Duke Kung. He was one of the very few hereditary nobility in China, to whom high honour is given, from the fame and influence of his great ancestor. He entered freely into conversation on various subjects; but he did not seem particularly intelligent. I spoke to him of Christ, and he listened respectfully, though the object of his visit was mere curiosity to see a foreigner, with whom he could hold intercourse in his own language.

I became acquainted with a Chinese scholar, who was the agent of the late Viceroy at Nankin, Tseng-Kwoh-fan. On one occasion, he brought to me the head of a small animal, which he said had been offered for sale as part of the spoils of the Emperor's palace. The sutures on it had astonished the Viceroy, and were pretended by some foreigner to be the handwriting of Buddha. I was asked if I could tell anything about them, and showed him a number of plates with the same impressions. This did not avail to clear up the mystery; but I recollected having similar bones in the house, and on laying them before him, with sutures of the same kind, he expressed himself indignant at his master having been imposed upon as he was, and at such a large price being sought for the skull of a mere old animal. This same scholar was a high-minded Confucian. He entered into conversation about Christianity, magnifying his ancient sage as far superior to Jesus Christ. I told him that there was no ground in the native classics for such a celebration of Confucius. A passage was adduced in which the sage confessed his shortcomings, and another showing that his conduct was not altogether truthful and honest. He was irritated in the extreme, and said, "If you say anything derogatory of our holy sage, let me tell you that I would rather go to hell with him, than with your Jesus Christ to heaven."

Two Mahommedans called on me one day, and expressed a desire to hear our Christian doctrine. They had come from a distance for the purpose. I said that I was glad to see them, and mentioned that our chapels were open daily for preaching; and invited them to come to my house any time for religious conversation. They were frequently present at the services. At the end of ten days, they visited me again, and as they were about to return home, they wished to thank me for my kindness during their stay in the neighbourhood. I assured them it was unnecessary, but desired to know what they thought of our preaching. They replied that Jesus was truly a wonderful man. He was wise and holy and good. They knew Him as one of their own prophets. His name in their pronunciation was *Urh-sa*. They said that if we would only go through the country, preaching about Christ, His goodness, His wisdom, and His miracles, we should get thousands of converts. I thanked them for their estimation of Him, but thought that there was something in their minds which they were hesitating to tell me. I encouraged them to speak out on the matter. After a time, they said it was true they had an idea on the subject, which they were afraid of expressing, lest it should give offence; but as I wished them to speak out, they would venture to do so. The idea was this,—they were surprised at my continually preaching about the cross, and that Jesus had died on it, as an atonement for human sin. They urged me to go everywhere speaking of Christ in His moral character and life, but never to say that He died on the cross. This was a thing which the Chinese were too proud to believe, and if persisted in, we should meet with no success in our work. I told them that this was the very kernel of our doctrine, and apart from it, I should never have come to China at all. There were moral teachers and systems in abundance amongst them; and in view of the spiritual condition and necessities of men, the death and atonement of Christ could not be dispensed with.

Our general preaching is curiously listened to by some of our audiences. When engaged in the open air, we are often asked strange questions, such as these, "What kind of coat is that you have on?" "What is the price of the cloth a yard?" "What are your shoes made of, and how long will they wear?" "Is your country far from this?" "How is it that you have a Queen and not a King reigning over you?" The productions of our country are often matters of inquiry, but of course we always endeavour to put aside such questions, though they are not to be wondered at as significant of the ignorance of the people, who have no idea of there being any impoliteness or impertinence connected with them.

I remember a Missionary preaching to a large audience, and on closing the service, a Chinaman went up to another of our number standing at the door, and entered into conversation with him. In the simplicity of my early days, I thought he was talking about what he had just heard, and on asking what he was saying, it turned out that the purport of his communication was to know if there were any moons in our country.

As an instance of mandarin peculation I may mention the following. Two of us were travelling in the interior, and were invited to the public office to stay for the night. It was a politic step on the part of the magistrate to do so, as he was apprehensive of the presence of foreigners in the city. He was an abandoned opium smoker, and was astonished to see us, never having fastened his eyes upon such beings before, and it was some time ere he could recover from his fright. In the course of general conversation, we told him about England, its high officers and emoluments. Particularly it was urged upon him, that they received a specified salary, and could not *lung* or manage for themselves to the extent of a single copper beyond it. He held up his hands in amazement, and said the mandarins of his country could never get on at all if they did not *lung*. It was necessary for their very existence. During the same journey we were entertained by another mandarin, who was a very intelligent man, and who expressed his satisfaction at what we told him of our country. When we spoke of the House of Commons, he looked at us with great earnestness, and said,—" that is what we want in China, a representation of the people in the capital, so as to put a stop to the many evils current in the land."

While continuing our course, we were reading an itinerary of the way, and the volume narrated the story of a priest who had lived on the top of a hill we were going to. It was called *Tien-muh*, or the eye of Heaven. This holy priest was walking along the brink of a precipice named the Tiger's Mouth, and was so absorbed in the contemplation of Buddha and the repetition of his prayers, that he fell over, but such was the wonderful merit he had acquired, that he sustained no injury. When found at the bottom, he was repeating with great composure the mystic words, *O-mi-toh-fuh*, which it was observed might well be rendered in the circumstances, O my toe and foot! These words are supposed to have an unspeakable worth connected with them. We have seen priests and hermits in particular, who appeared to utter them incessantly, thinking that the more frequently they did so, it would add vastly to their merit both in this world and the next. Sometimes men of that stamp are voluntarily incarcerated for years in a small room, never leaving it, while they occupy their time, day and night, in repeating the sacred symbols, and resounding the praises of old Buddha.

At the close of Dr. Medhurst's service in the chapel one Sunday afternoon, a Chinaman went to the pulpit and handed a small book to him, asking if he knew what it was about. It seemed to contain a number of figures or diagrams, and Dr. Medhurst requested him to call at his place next day. On examination, it was found to be a treatise on the higher mathematical calculus. The owner of it said it was the product of four years' arduous study. He was engaged by Mr. Wylie as a teacher, and prosecuted a course of mathematics with him for many years. He had a perfect genius for it, and experienced no difficulty in any department. He went through a work on Algebra, the latter nine books of Euclid, a Complete System of Trigonometry and of Differential and Integral Calculus. He translated Herschel's Outlines of Astronomy,

Whewell's Mechanics, and a variety of other scientific works, all in the easiest way possible, and showing a complete mastery of every subject. His anxiety was to translate Newton's Principia, and he is now occupied with or has lately finished it. He has been appointed in connexion with the Imperial Observatory, at Pekin, which he is far more capable of superintending than any of the other officials. The number of men qualified and capacitated as he is for mathematics and general science are few, but he was the means of bringing several into acquaintanceship with us. One of them was the governor of the important city of Suchow. I remember his calling at the Mission, when he was free from official duty for three years, according to Chinese custom, on the occasion of his mother's death. We conversed on various topics. He was much interested in the views of Astronomy that had recently been published, and he spoke of a similar work on Geology. In reference to the long eras required by that science, he said that they seemed to be more in keeping with the vast kulpas of the Buddhists, than the limited chronology of the Scriptures, and appeared to prove the truth of the one rather than that of the other. These men in general had no special drawing to Christianity. Much as they admired our scientific writings, they had no idea of conforming to our religious system, but carelessly held on to their own moral or materialistic creed.

Some time before leaving China I visited Japan, and was much interested in the sights and scenes of that beautiful land. I was hospitably entertained by the Rev. Mr. Verbeck, of the Dutch Reformed Mission. He was familiar with the native language, and was held in high respect by the people. Persons came to visit him from a distance. Amongst them was a Buddhist priest, whose single object was to learn Christianity. He had been studying it for a long time, and was familiar with its leading particulars. He had many difficulties to solve and many inquiries to make, and when any of these were satisfactorily answered, he noted the replies down, in order as he said, that he might tell them to his friends in the interior, who were similarly minded with himself. His Buddhism sat very lightly upon him. He stated that it was the recognized religion of the country. All were compelled to profess it from the time that Catholicism was prohibited, but he was persuaded that the religion as well as the science of the West would ultimately prevail. He thought it wise in common with many others of his cloth to become acquainted with the former, so as to be prepared for the times that were coming. He was told that Christianity was a spiritual system, affecting the heart and conscience, no less than the outward life, and his eyes were manifestly opening to the perception of the fact. Still he urged that so long as it was proscribed, it was inconvenient to change his Buddhist profession, but he would do so, and many more, when Christianity became the religion of Japan. This reminded me of a letter that I had shortly before received from a Japanese friend in Singapore. When about sixteen years of age, the junk in which he was sailing, was driven by a storm from the coast, and during eleven months was tossed about in the North Pacific. His companions nearly all died, and the vessel drifted upon the Western shores of America. He was taken by the American Indians, and kept among them for a time. At length he escaped to an English ship, and was brought to Hongkong. He was converted to Christianity through the labours of the late Dr. Gutzlaff. Subsequently he removed to Shanghai, where he lived for many years in a very consistent manner. He accompanied one or more of the expeditions to Japan as interpreter, and was in some danger from being looked upon as a renegade from his native country. When his health failed he went to Singapore, and at that time an embassy from Japan was on its way to England under Sir Rutherford Alcock. My friend met the members of the embassy, who asked him if he was a Christian, and he told them that he was. Their answer was this—"that they had long been striving to keep Christianity out of Japan, but they were persuaded it was impossible. The time would assuredly come when it would be tolerated and extend in the regions of the rising sun." This Japanese Christian died not long ago in the blessed hope of heaven through faith in Jesus Christ. My other Japanese acquaintance was of the opinion of the embassy, that our religion would finally prevail, and expressed much surprise on reading in our Chinese Bible the passage, that "from the rising of the sun unto the going down of the same, Jehovah's name is to be exalted." He presented me on leaving with a list of Christian books in Chinese, which he desired me to get for him, and I had the satisfaction of sending him eight hundred volumes of various kinds, which he duly paid for.

Many other incidents might be narrated in connexion with my prolonged stay in China, but these will suffice to show its general character and bearing. Cases of conversion among the men and women, young and old, might be detailed, but it is not my purpose to enlarge. The above will indicate our ordinary experience, and though the results of Mission work may not appear to be of great moment, or as yet affect the general condition of the country, yet we now see the beginning of the end. We are persuaded that the changes that have occurred during the last twenty years, are an index to still more marvellous changes in the future. The history of the next ten or twenty years in China politically, socially, and religiously, will be far more striking than that of the same period which has just passed away. The one has been only preparatory to the other; and however great the difficulties in the way, however opposed the Chinese are to improvements or innovations of any kind, they cannot resist the general progress of things, and events are destined to occur which shall change the face of the nation, and lay its heart open to all the influences brought to bear upon it. "Who art thou, O great mountain, before the servant of Christ, thou shalt become a plain."

CHAPTER VIII.

OBJECTIONS AND ANSWERS.

Various objections have been brought against our Missionary work in China, which deserve to be considered. They bear upon the present state of the field, the character or standing of the men engaged in it, and the mode of their operations. We do not expect sympathy or support from all our countrymen on the spot, but things are often said in regard to Missions which we deem it our duty to reply to. Some have been surprised at the statements thus currently reported, and though disposed in our favour at first, have been won over to the opposite side by the views so freely and frequently expressed. We are not about to vindicate the Missionaries as perfect men in their character or in their work, neither are we inclined to admit their great and grievous deficiencies, as is too commonly alleged, yet we think that the subject may be looked at in its own proper light.

We have heard it asserted that China is not prepared for the reception of the Gospel. The people are too proud or prejudiced, ignorant or superstitious, and they must be awakened and enlightened by means of Western science and civilization. Till then little hope is entertained by some of the progress of Christianity in the country. We have already said enough as to the introduction of our more advanced forms of culture in China. We hail every attempt of the kind as ancillary to the object we have in view. But surely it argues strangely for our Divine Christianity, if it must wait the accomplishment of the state of things here referred to. We admit that China has been opened through foreign influence, and in a way which we may not altogether approve of, but this has been happily overruled. Still the history of the past, the claims and character of our religion, and the terms of our Lord's commission are sufficiently instructive on this point. In ancient times, nations and tribes existed that were distinguished by all possible varieties of culture and civilization, and among them equally and alike the Gospel was preached with salutary effect. In modern times the same has been the case, and there is nothing in the intellectual or moral aspect of the Chinese that forms an exception to the rule. Jew and Gentile, Greek and Barbarian, were visited and converted in former days, and until the commission is revoked, we believe it to be of paramount and binding authority. Be the social and political condition of the Chinese what it may, the Gospel is as adapted to it as it is to other men, and even were it not, our duty in the matter would be no less imperative, while retaining the name of the followers of Christ. In a word, China has shown the capacity of being influenced by different and opposing systems of morals and religion, and it is our opinion that there are peculiar advantages connected with it in favour of the spread of the Gospel. We think it unnecessary to dwell longer on this topic, as every thoughtful inquirer will perceive the truth and propriety of what we have stated.

It has been said that the Gospel is presented to the Chinese in a very unsuitable form by the variety of Missionaries in the field. They are each supposed to advocate their different opinions, so as to be a cause of confusion to the people. We regret that this should be the case in any degree, but we do not believe that it is attended with so much injury as might be feared. The Missionaries are not in the habit of indoctrinating the Chinese with their peculiar or denominational views. Their work is to preach the Gospel, and they do it in as simple and earnest a way as they can. At the same time we wish that the barrier of denominationalism were removed to as great an extent as possible, and that it might not be even apprehended in this heathen land. We shall have occasion to refer to it in our next chapter.

A more frequent and formidable series of objections is drawn from the supposed character or standing of the men engaged in the Missionary work. Many of them are said to be incompetent for the position which they occupy, as heralds of the Gospel to such an enlightened and cultivated people as the Chinese are. Is it so in reality? What is the impression conveyed to the mind on looking over the list of Missionaries that have entered the field from the earliest times? Judge them by their works. Have not many of them from the first distinguished themselves in every department, as Chinese scholars, as devoted Missionaries, as well as Christian men? We will not descend to particulars. The writings and labours of these men are patent to the world, and have won for them the greatest admiration and honour. Is this not acknowledged in the case of such men as Morrison, Milne, Bridgman, Boone, Abeel, and Medhurst, not to mention others who have passed away, or who are still engaged in the field? But it is alleged that all are not of this class and standing. No, and could it be expected in the nature of things? Is it the case that in every position in life all are equally able and distinguished? Is not the great majority in every department of an inferior grade and character? And yet may they not be fitted as a whole for their own proper office and work? In the Missionary staff, as well as in the ministerial body at home, there is only the usual variety, and this no less in China than elsewhere. It is the same in spiritual as it is in secular things. It were unreasonable to expect it to be otherwise. It may be that men who are regarded as possessing the highest qualifications for Christ's service abroad, most generally prefer to remain at home. We will not impute any motive to them in the matter, but even if a lower standard really characterizes the Missionaries that are labouring in a heathen country, are they to be blamed for consecrating themselves to the work, when others refuse to embark in it? Nay, more than this, we hesitate not to take equal ground with the ministerial body in our native land, and are ready according to our measure to stand shoulder to shoulder, man for man, with our compeers in more favoured circumstances. Looking at our numbers, and the varied attainments of those connected with us, we are bold to say that we are in proportion not a whit behind our fellow-labourers in Christendom. Like the apostle, however, we deprecate this boasting, and would rather say that we are even at the best unworthy of our high calling. We magnify our office, not ourselves, and earnestly wish that men of the noblest standing, and purest piety, and greatest zeal and devotedness to Christ's cause among the heathen, would join us in our arduous undertaking. We are willing to be "hewers of wood and drawers of water" for the Lord's temple, and would gladly cede any position of honour that we occupy from the necessities of the case. It is not so much those in the field who ought to be charged with incompetency for the work, as others, it may be, better qualified, for refusing to engage in it at all. At the same time we maintain, that taking us all in all, we are neither better nor worse than our fellows, and the labours in which we have engaged, and the impressions that we have produced in China, as in other parts of the world, bear testimony in our behalf. Let those who are ever ready to bring up this objection against us, look to themselves, and compare their own degree of competence with others in like position. Are they perfect in their calling? Are they up to the mark on all occasions? Do they never commit mistakes? Are they warranted to speak of Missionaries whom they know little about, and who are doing what they can in their Master's service, in the absence of others more able, perhaps, or more willing to do it? Our counsel to such is, that their part is rather to aid, encourage, and advise the servants of Christ in their labours among the heathen, and who would gladly accept all the sympathy and support it is in their power to give.

Another thing commonly stated is that the Missionaries are idle in the discharge of their work, and are therefore unworthy of confidence and respect. If it is so, they are blameable in a high degree. They are not sent out with this idea, and they are not supposed to spend their time in indolence and inactivity. They are in this case unfaithful to their Lord and to the churches of which they are the messengers. Indolence in a Missionary is a crime of the deepest dye. But can it be reasonably charged against any of the class? We know not. One thing we do know that the majority of our countrymen around us are as ignorant of us in our Missionary work, as we are of them in their mercantile pursuits. There is little or no communication between us. We regret it on various grounds, and take our share of the blame connected with it. We should like to see a better understanding on both sides. We hope it will be ere long in China, as it is happily to a growing extent in India and other places. As to the charge, however, we will not speak unduly or beyond our knowledge; yet we do say that Missionary work has been prosecuted in China on the part of many with the utmost zeal and energy. They have lived and laboured intensely for the advancement of it. Whatever portion of the work has been assigned them, it has been done as they best could, though none are more prepared to admit than they, that all they have done is little compared with what they wish to do. The study of the language, the translation of books, the preaching of the Gospel, the superintendence of native churches, the education of youth, the healing of the sick, and the various duties of our sacred calling, have been attended to with no less ardour and assiduity than are to be witnessed among our compeers at home. We can say of numbers in the field that they have not spared themselves. Mission work has been their delight and passion. Their record is on high, whatever estimate may be formed of it on earth, and they are willing that it should remain there. Perplexed and overwhelmed they often are by the difficulties and discouragements of their work, and baffled at times as to the best means of carrying it on; yet we knowingly affirm that in their separate spheres of labour there are and have been Missionaries in China fully equal to the best, noblest, and most devoted ministers in their native land. There are diversities of gifts and activities it is true in the one case, as well as in the other, but on the ground of our own experience and observation we will not consent to the imputation we are now referring to. Of this we are assured, that those who are most accustomed to bring it against us at their convivial meetings, are the least qualified to do it, and their own habits of life are scarcely of a kind that warrant them making it at all. We might reasonably ask, what are they doing as Christian men for the conversion of the heathen? Are they under no obligation in the matter? A large Christian community like that now existing in China, might be expected to produce an impression upon those around it favourable to the cause of Christianity. Is this the case? Our well and widely known reputation as Missionaries among the heathen is a testimony on our behalf, that we have not lived a life of idleness and inactivity, and we trust that we have the moral sense rather to quit the field and cede our position to others, than indulge in a course fraught only with ignominy and guilt.

We are next charged with a want of the self-denial which it is thought should be an essential characteristic of a Missionary to the heathen. Certain ideas are formed with regard to him that do not exist in reference to a minister at home. Why it is so is a question which we leave others to determine. Simply because a man is disposed to embark on foreign work, so it is said he should relinquish all the privileges and enjoyments which would have been granted to him in his own country. He is expected to be ever on the move, and not to be encumbered or embarrassed by the cares of family life. Anything of this kind is looked upon as inconsistent with the full discharge of his Missionary work. The celibate is considered to be the proper order of the day, and so the Roman Catholic Missionaries are praised, while the Protestants are accused of enjoying themselves with their wives and children, and with all the comforts and conveniencies of home in a foreign land. We admit that there are often disadvantages belonging to such a mode of life, arising from the sickness of the members of a Mission family, as may be the case with the Missionary himself, whether he is single or married. But the point is this, does family life necessarily or ordinarily interfere with Mission work? Is the Missionary rendered less active and useful in consequence of such an arrangement? Can it be said of Ministers at home? We declare on the broad ground of twenty years' experience, it is not so on the part of Missionaries abroad. We have the record of Missionary life in many lands to sustain us in this statement. A Missionary is in no wise kept back from the diligent prosecution of his work by his home life among the heathen, any more than a Minister is in his native country, or than a merchant is in his peculiar calling abroad. If it is so, we unhesitatingly assert that he is not a man of the right stamp. We have in our view numbers of married Missionaries who carried on all the departments of their work in the neighbourhood and in the surrounding country, and were second to none of their unmarried brethren. Nay, they were more settled in mind, more arduous in effort, and more accustomed to travelling in the interior than many of the others. We do not insist upon the one kind of life rather than another. Let every man be persuaded in his own mind. Only it is wrong to say that married life is detrimental to Missionary work, when both parties are interested in the welfare of the heathen round about. The opposite idea arises from a complete misconception of the facts of the case, and is formed on the ground that a Missionary should be a paragon of self-denial in all manner of things; as if the more this was done, the more laborious and successful was he likely to be in his work. Will the objectors as Christian men voluntarily follow this course for themselves? It is thought that a Missionary should go into the interior, mingle with the people in their own homes, identify himself with them, and be separated from all the associations and enjoyments of civilized life. There are Protestant Missionaries who do this in certain places. But wherein is the practical advantage of it in China? Not long ago it was impossible to go into the interior at all, and even now it is a matter of question. Whether in the city or in the country, however, are there not sections of the community who may be influenced for good by the wife, as well as, or even better than by the husband? And seeing they have devoted themselves for many years to this one thing, why should they be enfeebled by the withholdment of the sympathy and support which they can tender to each other in the prosecution of their work? Is the celibate, is the self-denial spoken of to be required from the Missionary abroad? We insist upon its equal observance at home. If the separation from all ties of country and kindred is to be demanded in the one case, let it be also in the other. If the Roman Catholic life is necessary in foreign climes, it is no less so in Christian lands. We are aware of some of the miseries attendant upon isolation on the part of Romish Missionaries in China, and we deprecate it in the case of Protestants labouring there. Our idea is that Missionaries are not to be looked upon as peculiarly distinct from their ministerial brethren. They simply occupy another portion of the field, and, as devoted, earnest men, they will not necessarily allow anything to interfere with the corresponding prosecution of their work. Married life as a rule is not found to do so, and there is no reasonable cause for insisting upon it as a regulation of Mission service.

But in connexion with this, it is maintained that Protestant Missions are expensive in the salaries that are allowed, or in the houses that are occupied by them in a heathen land. Is it really so? What is the salary? In China the average is £300 to married Missionaries. Is this equal to what is given to many a young man in a mercantile situation? Our honoured predecessor, after forty years' of service, had this salary; but we know that little would be thought of it by persons either at the first, or after long engagement, in a mercantile capacity in the East. It is hinted that Romish Missionaries get much less, and that they are to be commended for it; but our salary is objected to as exorbitant, and as rendering Protestant Missions most expensive. Is this the statement of enlightened Christian Englishmen? Would the sum be found too large for their wants in such a country as China? Neither the Missionaries nor the Societies to which they belong, are careful about getting or giving too much in the way of salary. We have not undertaken the work on the ground of remuneration. The writer was not aware of his allowance until he was far away on the sea. It was stated in a sealed envelope, to be opened on board, and he has never regretted the arrangement. We only ask,—is the charge of the expensiveness of Protestant Missions in China of any real weight, considering the facts of the case? Is it consistent with health, or is it urged as a matter of necessity that they should be prosecuted on more economical and frugal terms? Should the Missionary be placed on a footing of equality, simply with the humbler portion of the heathen community, and be obliged to accommodate himself to their modes and habits of life? Is it the case with ministers at home? Is it the practice of merchants abroad? Is it true that Missionaries are so exceedingly comfortable and luxurious in their houses and family circumstances, that they can be charged as they have been? Let their salaries tell the tale. We know the difficulty of making ends meet, yet would gladly do with less were it found to be possible. We are thus minute in alluding to the matter, from the hints that have appeared in the public papers on the subject, and the inuendoes that have been thrown out in other quarters. In reply to them all, we have only to say, that it was from no idea or expectation of comfort, or indulgence or ease, that the Missionary work was contemplated by us or our fellow-labourers; and the expense of maintaining it as a representation of Bible Christianity in this vast heathen land, is little in comparison with many other interests of passing value and importance. We cannot think these hints and inuendoes are uttered by men who have any right knowledge of the state of matters. We despise them as anonymous publications. They are fitted to convey a totally wrong idea of things. We would esteem a frank and friendly interchange of sentiment about it; but to intimate that Missionaries are living in luxury and in the enjoyment of every comfort, is simply untrue, contradicted both by fact and the necessities of the case. If the standard of such writers is the right one, we trust that we shall have grace to follow it; but of course it must be equally right everywhere, and Christian men of all classes, lay and cleric, are equally under obligation in regard to it. We can only imagine, however, that the ideal of these writers is the monastic habit and customs of the native priests, or of Romish Missionaries at home and abroad; and in the face of all their insinuations, we simply decline to copy their example. We disclaim the one at the same time that we repudiate the other.

Doubts are thrown upon our work, from the supposed character of some of the converts. It has frequently happened that a number of Chinese young men, brought up in Mission schools at Singapore and other places, have been connected with foreign houses from their knowledge of English. Not a few of these have appeared to the merchants as of the lowest type, and hence the stigma that has often been thrown upon Mission work in general. But it is an unfair imputation. There are many young men in similar circumstances among ourselves. Even had these Chinese scholars been professing Christians, the temptations into which they were led by contact with foreign service, were of the worst kind; and as in other cases, had a baleful influence. Money was easily acquired in their new position, which introduced them into a circle of vicious companions; so it is not to be wondered at that many of them fell away and showed that their English education, which was all that they could boast of, was a means of harm rather than otherwise.

It seems to be expected by foreigners that converts from heathenism in China should all at once be perfect men, in spite of the evil associations of the past, and their inveterate national character. We ourselves are not what we are as the result of a brief period of Christian work; and it ought to be kept in mind, that it is only a few years since China was opened to Christian enterprise. Now, we cannot make bricks without straw, and we cannot in a short time make a Chinese convert the noble, intelligent, active, and spiritually-minded Christian, that we are aiming at. Still, it is not ours to talk of failure or discouragement, when we are engaged in Christ's service and in God's work. It is His from first to last. Unless we had this conviction, we should give it up. Whatever be the results of what we are doing, we are doing it only in obedience to His will, and are fired with zeal and devotedness only on this ground. Talk of failure in the Mission cause in China! It has been well said that it is the only cause which has been successful of late years. Mercantile operations have grievously failed. Many connected with them have speculated and lost. Our work is no speculation. Its success is guaranteed, and we have realized the fact in the number and character of our Christian converts, as well as in the openings secured to us for preaching the Gospel. We should rejoice in seeing a larger number of conversions, and a greater improvement in the moral character and intelligence of our people; but we thank God for the measure of blessing **that has** come to us, and regard it as the earnest of still better and nobler days. We believe that "the little one shall become a thousand, and the small one a great nation, for the Lord will hasten it in His time."

Some seem to think that our preaching is of little avail in the present condition of things. The idea is that China must be enlightened on the side of the upper classes in the first place, who will by-and-bye influence the lower, and thus the country will be Christianized. It is suggested, that as the scholars form the ruling element, they ought to be specially aimed at for a series of years, by some of the best men sent out for the purpose. These ought to be employed in mastering the language, in preparing lexicons and other works, which will be useful afterwards to a number of able, philosophic students from the West, who will succeed them in attacking the prevailing systems of the day, and exposing their absurdities. This is to end in the conversion of many of the native scholars. When this is the case, and they are convinced of the truth and superiority of our religion, they will in due time, it is supposed, bring about the similar conversion of those beneath them in the scale. We repeat that we have no objection to the employment of every available means for the enlightenment and improvement of this people. We should hail the services of such a class of men as that now spoken of, and would entreat those who have a sympathy in that direction to use their influence accordingly. But no consideration of this kind can move us away from what we believe to be the path of duty,—the public preaching of the Gospel to one and all, whether they will hear or whether they will forbear. We admit that the scholars of China are now our bitterest opponents, and that they exercise a dominant power in the country. We have a work, however, which has to do with men apart from their standing in society, and which requires to be done while we have opportunity. The foreign merchants pursue their avocations with those who come around them for the purpose; and following our Divine Master as well as the necessities of the case, we carry on our labours in the most public manner, and for the common good. Allow it that these scholars stand aloof and treat us and our message with contempt, it has always been so in the history of Christianity, until it gained for itself, by the very means we adopt, the respect and confidence of high and low, rich and poor, learned and unlearned. We should be glad of the adherence of many of the upper classes,—the wise, the noble, and the mighty of this world,— but they must come under the power of the truth in the same way as the others, instead of having their tastes pandered to in a special manner, and instead of being regarded as a privileged caste. We have men of this kind among us, and are thankful for them. We are hopeful as to a growing increase of their number, when all the influences now and afterwards at work shall have been more effectual, and the blessing of God shall descend more richly and abundantly upon our labours. We pray that education may be brought to bear in one way or another more fully on the Chinese, as is being done in India, and anticipate good results from it; but we cannot forego the preaching of the Gospel by the best means we can employ. We consider ourselves as mainly shut up to it in present circumstances, and are persuaded that the more we give ourselves to it, and increase in our qualifications for it, we shall, under God, fulfil the ministry that has been committed to us.

It has been lately said in high quarters, that Missionaries are the occasion of great trouble wherever they go, endangering the peace of the country, and are therefore denounced as "either enthusiasts or rogues." Such is the understanding and appreciation of their character and labours on the part of a certain noble Duke in the House of Lords. The worst construction has thus been put upon the Missionary work, as pursued by some of its agents. It is no new thing. We read of it in Apostolic times at the hands of the heathen, who had no sympathy with the servants of Christ. These were made a spectacle to the world. They were regarded as the offscouring of all things, and treated accordingly. But to hear such a statement made by a nobleman professing Christianity in these days, may well astonish us. Doubtless it was uttered by him, from the idea that Missionaries were imprudent in their movements among the heathen, and so causing grievous offence, while they relied on the protection of their native country. We believe they are entitled to that protection, according to the stipulations of the treaty; and His Grace shows very little knowledge of its terms, or the bearing of Missionary work, or the character of the Chinese in relation to it, by the manner in which he talks. We disclaim the charge evidently implied in the above expressions. We do not consider that we are either so wild or so wicked as to deserve it; and we are not in the habit of appealing for gunboats, either for our personal safety or for the propagation of the Gospel. We ask no more assistance or protection than would be ceded to any subject of Her Majesty living in China, and observing the stipulations that have been made by treaty. It is in this capacity alone that any assistance or protection has been sought and obtained; and it is not as Missionaries, but as foreigners, that it has ever been found necessary. In carrying out our work, however, we beg to tell the Duke of Somerset, that we are called upon to be "enthusiasts" in the best and noblest sense, for without such a spirit we shall do little good, and make little impression in the world. It is indispensable as an element of Missionary life and character, and we pity the man who has none of it. We thank the Duke for the term as we are disposed to understand it, and only wish that we were more possessed of the thing itself. On the other hand, we do pity him for the epithet of moral delinquency, which he has dared to affix to the Missionary name, as if it were even a possible fact.

Finally, we hear it stated that the Gospel is making comparatively little way in China, from our preaching largely on the subject of eternal punishment. This has astonished us on many grounds. Of course, were it true, it equally applies to the general preaching of the Gospel at home. We are not aware of any specialty in this respect in China, compared with other places. There is no difference in the truths we preach, in the character of the people who hear them, or in the effects produced by them. If there is any new Gospel to be proclaimed, let us know its claims, its import, its advantages. If we are chargeable with not preaching what is understood by the Gospel of Christ, let the accusation be brought forward and substantiated. Or if the Chinese are particularly susceptible on the point of being called to suffer for their sins or their unbelief, and on this ground refuse to accept the offer of Divine mercy and forgiveness, let us understand the fact, that we may act upon it.

We are aware of certain views being propounded in reference to the eternity of future punishment and the annihilation of the wicked. Are we guilty of insisting on the opposite ideas? and are we therefore to be blamed as the means of hardening the heathen mind against the Gospel? If there is the slightest ground for the charge in our case, it may be alleged with equal force of the preaching that has been carried on in all past time. Be this as it may, we do not plead guilty in the matter, notwithstanding the authority of a certain high official, formerly in China, on the point. If rash statements are occasionally made about Confucius, by any of the Missionaries, it is the exception, not the rule; and we can testify to the prudence and propriety of the Missionaries in general, in their preaching and in their public labours. We desire to overflow with love and pity for the multitudes around us, and to enter into the sympathizing and forbearing spirit of our Divine Master, while we are faithful in the proclamation of His solemn truth. We are compelled in the course of our work to make our hearers aware of their awful responsibility. Their acceptance or rejection of the Gospel message is declared by us to be fraught with most solemn consequences,—their own acceptance or rejection at last. They are familiar, however, with this aspect of things, in connexion with their own heathen systems, while we are sustained in it by the teachings of the Bible and the example of its messengers in all ages. We account for the continued unbelief of the Chinese, and no less of the people at home, by other causes than the one alluded to,—namely, by the ordinary depravity of the human heart, aided and abetted by the searing influence of heathenism.

For the conversion of the heathen we are driven to the necessity of special Divine grace. Shortly before leaving home there was a controversy existing on the subject of faith, as capable of being performed with the measure of grace usually accorded to every one. Ministers were to put forth their utmost powers in the matter; and "human suasion" in this way was said to be all that was needed. I was asked by one who had long been a Missionary abroad, what my opinions were on the

point. I mentioned them, and his reply was,—
" that it was all very well to talk of 'human suasion' in a Christian land, but when you get among the heathen, you will find it of little avail, do what you may, and you will be compelled to look to the special blessing of the Holy Spirit, as the alone effectual agency, in the conversion of those around you." This we express as our deepest conviction; and while striving to preach the Gospel in all its fulness, freeness and grace, we have often felt the truthfulness of these words,—" Not by might, nor by power, but by my Spirit, saith the Lord of Hosts."

CHAPTER IX.

REQUIREMENTS AND APPEALS.

The work we have been contemplating has one object in view, which may be expressed in three words—China for Christ. The vastness and grandeur of this idea cannot be sufficiently apprehended. It is to be measured by the greatness of the country, the immensity of the population, their present state of ignorance and error, and the consequent glory and blessedness of their conversion to Christ.

We are warranted to engage in this noble pursuit, by the assertion of His universal supremacy. "All power is given unto Me in heaven and on earth;" by His command to His disciples—"Go ye, therefore, and teach all nations;" and by the assurance of His gracious presence; "And lo! I am with you alway, even unto the end of the world."

Ancient prophecy is also teeming with promises of success in connexion with Christ's cause and kingdom, and there is one that seems specially to bear on China, while it includes all other parts of the earth. "Behold, these shall come from far, and lo! these from the north and from the west, and these from the land of Sinim."

Such passages of holy writ enter into the very spirit and essence of Christianity. It cannot be regarded apart from them, and the glowing anticipations that they contain. Its great and glorious truths are confirmed by the prospect of their ultimate universal extension, and the difficulties that have long stood in the way will only render their final accomplishment the more wonderful and triumphant.

Already we see indications of the end, in the openings that are taking place in the world at large, and that are being made subservient to the spread and growing power of the Gospel. The slow and gradual progress of Divine truth was foretold at the commencement. It was intimated that it should encounter many trials and drawbacks, both from without and from within the pale of its professors. All that has happened in regard to it has been in thorough accordance with the teachings of its Great Founder. Not a word that He spoke on the subject has failed all through the ages, whether in the way of apparent success or of defeat, and we take this as an evidence of the full and perfect completion of all that He has said about it. We may be impatient in the matter, and cry in the agony of our souls,—"O Lord, how long?" We are baffled to understand the Divine mystery, in the general economy of things. But it is ours to believe in the final issue, come when and how it may. We need not be perplexed. We have the promise of this world's regeneration and salvation. The means and agency connected with it are prescribed. The course of Providence is pointing to the same result, if not with the brightness of noon-day, at all events with the glimmer of the morning dawn; and we cannot observe the occurrences that are taking place in the earth at the present time, without cherishing the anticipation of the final triumph of Christianity. The best, the highest, the eternal interests of the human race are bound up in this destined issue, as they are most clearly and fully represented in the proclamation of gospel truth. No other system is to be compared with it in this respect. Its bearing on the individual and the nation is of the noblest kind. It places them high in the vantage ground. It elevates them to a foremost position among those around them, and thus attests its origin and results by the effects that it produces.

We are intent upon the diffusion of Christianity in China. We seek the moral and spiritual enlightenment of its hundreds of millions of people, their deliverance from the evils and the errors of idolatry, superstition and sin, and their enjoyment of the blessings of a full and a free salvation. We are encouraged to hope that the scheme is not utopian. Our past efforts have been crowned with a measure of success. It is ours simply to prosecute them to the end, in a manner that shall be adequate to the occasion. For this purpose there are certain elements required, on which we beg most earnestly to insist, and which we now proceed to notice.

In the first place, WE WANT MORE TIME FOR THE ATTAINMENT OF THE END IN VIEW.

The work in which we are engaged is a great and arduous one. We aim at the overthrow of a gigantic system of sin and evil, that has not only the natural depravity of the human heart to sustain it, but the hereditary deadening influences of many ages on its side. The whole order of things in China is arrayed against us. All that is usually said of a heathen country, in its opposition to Christianity, may be urged in full force in regard to the country before us. Its very enlightenment and civilization are transformed into a mountain barrier, and a thousand influences are at work to confront the message and the messengers of salvation. Can we expect all this to be overcome at once, or within the compass of a few years? The period in which we have been actually engaged is very brief. Few comparatively have been able to do good and efficient service, and however mighty, through God, the weapons of our warfare may be, they require to be wielded many a time, before the strongholds with which we are contending will fall to the ground. We are thankful for the victories already won, for the converts to the truth already gained. They are anticipatory of the success finally awaiting us, and all things considered, they are in full proportion to the attainments that have been made in other parts of the Mission field.

But we ask for more time in order to the complete accomplishment of our work. It were unreasonable to be discouraged, in view of the period we have been labouring, by the results that we have reaped. We did not undertake the work on the supposition that it was to be soon or easily effected. We are forbidden the entertainment of such an idea. We cannot tell how long we shall have to wait, but the history of the past informs us that centuries often elapse before the end comes, and a nation is converted to the truth. We do not think that this will be the case in China. Events are now thickening and conspiring in regard to it, which will hasten the downfal of the Confucian philosophy, and the errors of Buddhist and Taouist superstition. However this may be, that downfal is certain, and the means are in operation for the purpose. Only let us be persuaded of the rectitude of our cause, and though called to exercise patience, as in many other things, we are assured of the promised issue.

We may wonder at the necessity of more time, indefinite time, prolonged time, it may be, for its accomplishment, but such is the economy under which we are placed, and it has solemn and important lessons connected with it. If any are under the impression, that China is to be converted in a few years, and are acting accordingly, it were well for them to be disabused of the idea. Still if it should come about speedily, it will the sooner form an occasion of thanksgiving and praise. The fact is, however, we have nothing to do with the time at all. We are called to labour, and to believe that we shall not labour in vain, only "the end is not yet." It may be postponed for ages. Be it so, meanwhile duty is ours, and we are persuaded that when the end does come, China shall share in the joy of the nations, and in the gladness of a renovated world.

Next, WE WANT MORE MEN AND MEANS FOR THE ADEQUATE PROSECUTION OF OUR WORK.

This is a trite and ordinary observation in all departments of Christian service. "There is a post for every man, but not a man for every post." It must be acknowledged that China has attracted much attention at home since the opening of it, and not a few Missionaries have gone thither from different countries and sections of the Christian church. The world is everywhere calling for labourers as if the fields were whitening, and the harvest required to be gathered in. It is not to be expected, perhaps, that the demand can be fully met in the present condition of things. We are thankful for the measure of interest actually taken in, and of effort actually put forth, for the spread of the Gospel in foreign parts. Be the outcry aga'nst it in certain quarters what it may, we are glad that the various agencies in operation are sustained as they really are, in view of the circumstances of the case. But this is no reason for self-satisfaction and supineness in the future. Imperfect though the state of the church is in Christian lands, there is still a blessing in it, which needs to be quickened and stimulated for high and holy action both at home and abroad. A nobler form of Christian life is required on the part of one and all connected with it, that they may rise to the exigencies of the occasion, and do their part as "the salt of the earth and the lights of the world."

We have no new scheme to propose, but simply to urge the increased influence of the old Divine motive and consideration—THE LOVE OF CHRIST. Were this more effectually felt, it would lead to deeds of personal and united consecration that would tell mightily on the work before us. This principle indeed is necessary in all departments of religious service. It must sanctify and ennoble every effort in which we engage. Without it, such effort is poor and feeble, and wants the element which gives to it life and energy, moral excellence and power. The more it possesses and fires the soul, it brings us into sympathy with Him in whose spirit it originally breathed, and who was led by it to live and die for the salvation of a perishing world. All we want is correspondence to Him in this respect, and though at best it can only be in humble measure, yet in this way we shall walk in His footsteps, and overflow with pity and concern for sinful men. We need to be possessed of the love of Christ, to know and feel it to a greater degree, that we may be filled with all the fulness of God, and exemplify in action the fulness of Him who filleth all in all.

But we have specially to appeal to those who are looking forward to the Christian Ministry as the work of their life. We take it for granted that they are animated by the same holy and constraining motive, and would only plead with them to ask at the throne of grace,—" Lord, what wilt Thou have me to do?" His field is the world. He has charged His servants to go everywhere preaching the Gospel. No one assuming this office can forego the consideration as to what the Master would have him to do. It is not a matter of simple choice, but of solemn, sacred duty; and the man who enters upon the work of the ministry, without the serious, prayerful consideration of this subject, is lacking in a most important element of ministerial life and character. At the same time we lay it down as one essential qualification for Christ's service equally at home and abroad, that a holy burning zeal should inspire the soul in regard to it. And the direction, the tendency of that inward fire may be viewed as a test and proof of the will of

God in the matter. No man is at liberty to enter upon Christ's work unless he is thus impelled to it; and Missionary work in particular calls for all the energy and earnestness and enthusiasm of which the soul is capable. Conscience or moral principle is no doubt the first requirement, but no less must there be an intense, ardent solicitude in the spirit of that man who would go forward in the service of Christ anywhere. Without it, he will be of little worth, and reflect little credit upon the cause. A divine and heavenly inspiration is indispensable on the part of the Minister and the Missionary alike. It can be breathed into them only by the Spirit of God, and it is to be fostered and maintained by the highest and holiest aspirations.

What then as it regards the Missionary work? Its obligations are allowed. What are the claims which it has upon those who are training and offering themselves for the work of Christ? The number of these is considerable. Hundreds and thousands are preparing for it year by year in the different seminaries of our native land. What is their prevailing expectation and design? Is it not labour at home? And what is a frequent condition of things there? Numbers of small churches or congregations are to be met with, which make no progress in the onward course of time, and have a severe struggle for very existence. They find it hard to defray the current expenses of their religious worship, and ministers and people are borne down and crushed by the circumstances of the case. What is a leading cause of this in our estimation? The willingness of many of our young men to go to such places—to be satisfied with such a miserable kind of thing, rather than embark on the noble work of preaching the Gospel in the high places of the field, and compel a few Christian people to merge their individuality in the common fellowship of those around them. It is in our view a pitiful sight that thus everywhere meets the eye in a Christian land. We urge young men to be noble and worthy in their aspirations to carry out their Master's work. If they are fitted only for such humble and limited spheres of action, it is well that they should be left to occupy them, but we are satisfied that many deserve higher and better things, and they wrong both themselves and the cause by being content with them. Or is it that all are contemplating useful and honourable positions in the Church at home, and think these are no less necessary, while they are more in their line than foreign work? We answer that the home ministry must be provided for, but there is by no means such occasion for thinking of its claims and necessities in the present order of things, as there is of the exigencies of the heathen world. The command of Christ is as imperative as it ever was, and it is specially addressed to those of whom we are now speaking. The call from Heaven is as applicable to them as it was to the prophet in ancient times,

"Whom shall I send, and who will go for us?" May we not say, too, that the call from China and other places now is as loud and urgent to them, as was the voice of the man of Macedonia to Paul, "Come over and help us." What is the response which our aspirants for the Christian ministry give to these burning appeals? Are they listened to with the earnest and prayerful attention that they demand? Is it not largely taken for granted that they have no practical bearing upon them? Has it not been already resolved in numerous instances, as a matter of course, that home life is the life for them? It has its comforts, its ease, its emoluments in greater measure than foreign work. There are a thousand attractions in it that do not obtain in a heathen land. The climate, the language, the associations, the kind of work to be done,—these are all opposed to their ideas and wishes; while a stated ministry, a large and loving congregation, and a course of usefulness in the neighbourhood, are sufficient inducements for them to remain at home! How different is it in the case of many young men who, with a view to improve their position in life, eagerly embrace the opportunity of going abroad and stay there for a number of years. We will not allow that their circumstances are to be envied in comparison with ours. In many respects we maintain that ours are preferable, and it is on this account that we are often spoken against by those who think us possessed of superfluities to which as Missionaries we have no right. Be this as it may, we have to tell our youthful students and others, on the ground of personal experience and observation, that they have little to fear from the climate to be encountered, or the language to be learned, or the work to be done as Missionaries, if they have an ordinary share of health, an average measure at least of intellectual ability, and a burning desire to serve Christ, wheresoever He sees best in His Providence to send them.

The case of China has been described. The vast population, the openings we have into the country, the mastery we have obtained of the language, the facilities we enjoy in preaching the Gospel, and the success that has been already reaped,—all present an urgent plea and reason for more men and more means to be consecrated to the work. The number of Missionaries in China from different countries amounts to 166, besides 23 female missionaries, and 865 native assistants of all kinds. We are thankful that so many are engaged in the field. They form a great increase to the number in our own early days. Many of the missionaries have been labouring from fifteen to thirty and thirty-five years. They have enjoyed, on the whole, good health and vigour, and have not found the climate or the work in anywise injurious to them. In view of the vast extent of the country, however, we are compelled to ask, what are we among so many? Not a few of the Missions have a very minimum of men connected with them, and even if all on the list were capable of great and noble service, they are immensely disproportionate to the requirements of the case. Much more is to be done, and its performance as well as the general results of Mission labour in China, depends, under God, on a sufficient supply of men and means to do it.

The fact is that success at the different Mission stations appears to be in keeping with the number and efficiency of the labourers engaged. We observe on examining the statistics, that where the foreign Missionaries or native assistants are many, the results are of a corresponding kind. Of course the expense of maintaining these is in proportion, and it only shows that Mission work is not to be carried on in a stinted manner or with limited means, if it is wanted to be eminently successful. It is the same in this department of Christian service as in other things, equally at home and abroad. The increase of an agency will in general be attended by adequate results, but the diminution or minimum employment of it will be followed by like effects. "He that soweth sparingly shall reap also sparingly; and he that soweth bountifully shall reap also bountifully." We urge the serious consideration of this point in the matter of Christian Missions. While insisting on all proper economy being exercised in the conduct of them, we counsel no less the display of liberality answering to the greatness of the end in view, to the important bearing of it on the element of success, and to the course adopted in our most prosperous churches at home. The expense and voluntary agency connected with any one of these may well be taken as an example of what is required for the support of a great and influential cause in a heathen country.

We appeal on this ground for the enlarged and efficient maintenance of the Missionary work. We appeal to the merchants interested in the progress and development of China, and in the profits connected with its trade and commerce, that they may aid in this high undertaking. Why should not their gains be consecrated in some measure to the work—the moral and spiritual enlightenment of the millions of China? Their influence, their counsels, their sympathy in such a matter, would be eminently useful and becoming, as they are actually on the spot, and acquainted in some degree with the facts of the case. What should hinder this union of the lay and the clerical elements in the foreign as well as in the home field? Both would be benefited by it. There has been too much estrangement and separation between us in time past. We wish that both classes were identified in the Missionary undertaking, feeling a common interest in it, and helpful to each other in promoting its success. We appeal to the students of the Christian Ministry and others, that they will calmly and prayerfully consider the claims of China upon their services and labours, and be prepared to do the Master's will, in the language of the prophet,—"Lord, here am I, send me." O for for a fiery baptism of this kind among our young men, to qualify and constrain many of them to give themselves to Christ and His cause, not regarding their own comfort and advantage in the matter, but the glory of their Divine Lord and the spread of His Gospel in the world! We appeal to every branch of the Christian Church, and to every individual member of it, that they may rise to a proper sense of their dignity and duty in view of the work thus given them to do, —that they may act their part in regard to it, and by sharing in the intermediate labours, they may be entitled to rejoice in the ultimate issue, when "all nations shall call the Redeemer blessed."

Again, WE WANT MORE UNION AND CO-OPERATION AMONG THE MISSIONARIES ENGAGED IN THE FIELD.

We have no special scheme to propose under this head. It were perhaps foolish and useless to attempt it. The Church is largely divided at home, and there is every likelihood of its being so abroad. Still there is cause for rejoicing in the hearty, spiritual fellowship existing between the followers of Christ in all lands, apart from their various differences in external things. The one counterbalances the other to a great degree, and both are unspeakably better than any mere dead or dull uniformity. We willingly add our testimony to this state of matters in China. The Missionary brethren there are for the most part united in the truest and happiest sense. We feel that we are one in Christ and in His cause. We entertain the deepest respect and esteem for each other, and the differences between us are not allowed to interfere with our social intercourse, our Missionary conferences, or our meetings for prayer. In some cases, too, the converts of our several churches assemble together at stated times for united worship and service, which are conducted by one or other of the native brethren, according to their own mutual arrangement. All this is very gratifying, and shows that there is much Christian cordiality in our respective Missions. It is probable the utmost that can be expected in the present condition of things, and we are extremely diffident as to even suggesting any greater degree of union that might be gone into between them. The fact is, however, that there are denominational and other differences existing in China as elsewhere, which may be obstructive to our work, and which seem to us might be somewhat modified in action, with a measure of advantage to the common cause.

We do not suppose any of our Missionary brethren are in the habit of inculcating their particular opinions upon their converts, but it is undoubtedly the case that they are acted upon, and so they speak louder than words. There are fully twenty-five different societies, or denominations, or Missions represented in China, and we rejoice at it, in so far as they increase the number of labourers, and express the wide-spread interest of the church at home in the work. But is there no reasonable objection to the separated, disjointed aspect of the Missionary body, as it is thus comprised? Ought it to exist in this particular form? Is it the best and wisest system that could be devised and brought into operation? Does it not prove a source of weakness, instead of being, as the presence of so many Missionaries in the field would seem to imply, an element of mighty strength? What is the burden and bearing of our Lord's intercessory prayer? Union in the fullest sense of the term. What is the complaint brought against the Corinthian church? They were divided into sects and parties, which morally and numerically weakened and degraded them. What is required by the necessities of the case in China? That all the Missionaries there should be as closely ranged together as possible against the common foe, and employ all the means in their power for the edification and union of their adherents. But what is the condition of things in this respect? In some places, a number of small churches have been formed corresponding to the variety of denominations represented by the various Missions. The natives connected with them are led to entertain the peculiar prejudices and prepossessions, which mark the foreign Missionaries as a result of their home education. The style of things current among ourselves, in matters that are by no means essential, forms a distinguishing badge of the converts lately reclaimed from heathenism, and so the exact counterpart of our different sects and denominations at home is in danger of being observed and manifested abroad.

Our idea is that there should be nothing of this kind at all, that there should be a united church in China, and that there should be a common native development, adapted to the wants and circumstances of the place. We would carry this out to the utmost possible extent, considering that our great work as foreign Missionaries is to preach the Gospel, and not to organize the churches that might be gathered together, in a manner the most conformable to the varied state of things in the West. Ought not our Christian converts to have the right of adjudicating on this point, and to have the opportunity of determining their adherence to or union with each other in the fellowship of the church? We believe that they would soon settle, and settle well, many of the knotty matters that have so long, and so grievously separated Christians here. They have not the slightest sympathy with them, and we are not called upon to teach them on the subject, either by precept or example. We were once talking with an eminent native pastor about it, and asked him if he and his associates did not think that a union of all the Christians in the neighbourhood would be a good thing? His answer was to the following effect. "We should rejoice at it, but there must be some strange principle of separation between the foreign Missionaries, keeping them apart from each other, which we neither understand nor appreciate, and until a union is effected betwixt them, we must remain as we are."

The influence which our various ecclesiastical differences have upon us is necessarily reflected upon those over whom we are placed in the ministry. They look at and feel towards each other in a manner corresponding to what we ourselves do, allowing of course for the greater imperfection of their Christian character, and the greater lack of sympathy and spiritual unity in their case as compared with ours.

We are of opinion, however, that the whole tends to weaken the energies and impair the vital warmth of our Christian converts in Divine things. While they are only a few in number, divided into sects and parties, however real and genuine their religious life may be, there cannot be that fervour and animation, that zeal and confidence, that boldness and activity, which there might reasonably be in union and association with one another. We have often witnessed this in concerts for prayer and mutual exhortation held amongst them.

They always regard these seasons as high days in their experience. They are literally called "the great sabbaths for worship." This may be in accommodation to the Roman Catholic festivals, which are spoken of in this way, as distinguished from more ordinary occasions. Only such is the manner in which they look at these stated periods for united worship, and which we do not believe would be weakened in propriety or force were they more frequently observed. So long as the converts see and feel themselves a small body, separated from each other by various adventitious causes, which they cannot rightly apprehend, they are consciously "a feeble folk." They have no special interest in the other Christian denominations that are forming around them; and there is not that unity or concentrated action amongst them which there might otherwise be. They belong to this, that, or the other church, and they have little in common with those that are not of the same persuasion as themselves.

Now we deprecate all this kind of thing, and confess to no sympathy with it whatever. Some may plead expediency, and even moral and Christian principle in defence of it. From our standpoint, we urge the same motives and considerations, with at least equal power on the other side. We regard it as unseemly that Missionaries who have the same object in view, and the prosecution of it by the same great means, should be separate and apart from one another in their work, or in their churches, or in their fellowship. They have no opposing or selfish interests to serve by this arrangement. Whatever their convictions or impressions may be on the points on which they differ, they are of no value or importance in the matter of salvation, or compared with the welfare and progress of the cause they have on hand. And it is acknowledged that the union or association of the churches, under a form and order which they recognize as adapted to their circumstances and wants, would be most in harmony with the requirements of the case, and most promotive of the spiritual interests of those concerned. The converts would be thus brought together and trained for effectual and common action, while the support of their religious worship, and the native diffusion of the gospel would be more easily raised by their being united, than by their being kept apart.

A short time before the writer left his Mission field, all the members of the different churches were convened, and as the services were going on, the thought occurred to him that there is much talk at home about the self-support of the Missions abroad, and that as far as that field was concerned, there was the material for it before him. The converts were sufficiently numerous to undertake the charge of all the native pastors and teachers that might be required, whose election of course would be made to devolve upon them. In this way the church or churches would sooner become self-sustaining, than they could possibly be in a separated or divided state, while they would present a power in the midst of the heathen, far greater in the one case than in the other. As for the Missionaries, fewer would be required in a particular field by this system than now. Instead of all being needed for the superintendence or edification of several native churches, and the occupation of the surrounding districts, many of them would be set free to evangelize the country at large, or engage in other work, for which they might be better fitted, and in which they might be more useful.

But the question is, how could such an arrangement be carried out, even were it to commend itself to the judgment of experienced men? We suggest that the Societies or churches at home should give their Missionaries a degree of liberty and latitude to organize a scheme of the kind in their respective fields of labour. If the Missionaries are impressed with the necessity and propriety of it, on its own account, and from their fewness in any particular field, let them enter on its consideration with all grace and dependence on the Spirit of God. Let their only idea be the glory of their Divine Master, and the best interests of His cause and kingdom around them. Let some of their number be assigned the especial charge of the church or churches in the neighbourhood, leaving to the native teachers or pastors as much of the work as possible for the instruction of their fellow converts, while they might take an active and leading part in the general preaching of the Gospel and other elements of Mission labour. No change of course would take place in their personal relation to the churches or Societies at home. There would be ample occasion for the continued maintenance of that relation in the onward progress of the work. Our single idea at present is the organizing and consolidation of the native churches, so that they might be independent of all foreign interference or control, and that they might not be any longer regarded as in connexion with various churches or Societies in the West, beyond holding Christian intercourse with them. We are persuaded that such a state of things is by no means difficult of attainment in many quarters, where according to the present system, there is reserve, dependence, weakness, and discouragement. Our remarks, of course, especially apply to fields in which there are several Missions that are feebly sustained in respect of men and means, and that are unable in consequence to do any great and serviceable work.

Some may be surprised at the utterance of such opinions on the part of the writer, notwithstanding the well-known circumstances of the Mission field. It may be so, but it strikes him as a far more feasible plan for economising resources and forming Missions abroad, on an independent footing, than some other schemes that are now afloat. We will allow that it would require a change in the condition of things at home,—a higher order of spiritual life and piety, an intenser zeal and devotedness for the spread of Gospel truth—a merging of ecclesiastical differences and tastes in the concerns of Mission work,—and a willingness in the case of those engaged in it, to be anything and to do anything that God may be more abundantly glorified. This we confess to be a chief difficulty in the matter. Some are so attached to their peculiar order of church government, others are so distrustful of their fellow labourers, and all, it may be, are so accustomed to the state of things as they are, that there is no likelihood of common and united action in the grand scheme of evangelizing the world, and of working together for its attainment on the broadest scale. Still we do not withhold the utterance of these ideas. We are convinced that their ratification will come one day, when all our ecclesiastical dogmas,—the mode of baptism itself included,—will give way before the single determination of the whole Church to preach Christ and Him crucified to perishing men. As this feeling gains ground, as the love of Christ constrains us to follow His steps, so the present separating elements among His people will be borne down, and the prayer of our Lord be fulfilled, in their becoming one, even as He and His

Father are one, in the work of the world's salvation.

If this view is at all Scriptural and proper, might it not be pressed on the attention of Missionaries in the field, or enter into the conduct of Missions to be established on common ground in the future? If it is in accordance with the will and teaching of our blessed Lord, its realization greatly depends on the men who are placed in concert with each other in the great enterprise. Their sympathies with, and approval of, the scheme are indispensable to its being carried out, not in the way of a mere general friendship, but to the extent of hearty and efficient co-operation. Might we ask the question, what if the Church were united at home would be the bearing and aspect of the Missionary cause abroad? And what in a Christian point of view should hinder its union abroad, whatever be the impediments in the way at home? What have we to do with these impediments in the carrying out our great commission? They have nothing at all to do with us. They are of a merely local and temporary kind in their application and origin. They are, in our view, light as the dust of the balance, and of no more worth in the scale.

It is a Missionary that is uttering these ideas, and they may be looked upon as utopian and impracticable in the very nature of things. He is, however, differently minded, and states them as the result of long observation and experience in the field. It is his solemn conviction that by such means far greater work could be done abroad, and far greater economy exercised at home; while the care of the native churches, which often forms such a burden to the Missionaries and to Missionary Societies, would be more readily transferred to themselves, and be managed and determined accordingly. In this connexion, too, we may remark that newly arrived Missionaries would be thrown at once into a sphere of action of mighty consequence to themselves. We have seen such often at a loss as to how to proceed in their work, and time has been frittered away which might have been usefully and honourably employed, by their being placed in such an association as we have pointed out. It would stimulate and direct their energies from the first, and make them feel that they belong to a great institution, in which they would ere long be called to fulfil their part. May we say, further, that it might have the beneficial effect also of showing the churches at home the small value and importance of their various ecclesiastical differences, from these being borne down and neglected in the case of earnest men, and of infant churches in heathen lands. We feel as if we had neither time nor sympathy nor occasion for such things, in view of the momentous work given us to do, and the very dissimilar circumstances in which we are placed.

We have thrown out these hints and suggestions, fully expecting that they will be controverted by some, for whose opinions we entertain the greatest respect. They may be regarded both as unnecessary and as impossible of accomplishment. We have only to observe that if the present system is the best that can be devised, and most in accordance with the Master's will, we hope it will be carried out to the end. Our plea for union in the Mission field is simply from a desire to see our beloved work organized and its operations conducted in the most efficient manner,— for the glory of God and the salvation of souls.

Again, WE WANT MORE SYMPATHY AND INTERCOURSE BETWEEN THE MISSIONARIES AND THE CHURCHES AT HOME.

We are the messengers of the Churches. We have been deputed by them. We are their representatives in heathen lands, and are thus placed in special circumstances in relation to them. This connexion cannot be broken by any peculiar arrangement, such as Missionary Societies or Committees or Boards. These are useful and necessary in the administration of things, but they are not to be regarded as separating the Missionaries from the Churches of their native land. They are at best only the means of intercourse, and if they tend to keep the Missionaries distinct from the Churches at home in anywise, we cannot but look upon it as a disadvantage to both. We maintain the principle that we are in the closest association as Missionaries with all the Churches, and everything should be done to foster that connexion, to give strength and tenacity to it, and to keep alive the feeling of warmest sympathy in the matter. Our experience in England has been to the effect that much kindly feeling exists on the part of many of the Churches towards the Missionaries. They are welcomed on their return, and in such a way as awakens the impression, that if there were greater intercourse between them and the Churches in general, advantage of the highest kind would accrue to the Missionary cause. We feel our need of it in the field, separated as we are from the fellowship of Christian friends, and exposed to the depressing effects of heathenism.

We are thankful for the intervening agencies that have been established for the efficient conduct of our Christian work, and which have done such good service in time past, but our object is to enlist the deepest sympathies of the Churches, by a more direct correspondence on their part with the Missionaries abroad. There are many things connected with us which it would be useful for them to know, and which we have no occasion to communicate according to the present system. Without interfering with it in the slightest degree, we are inclined to think that if such a correspondence were opened, it would be the means of intensifying the missionary spirit of the Churches, making them more acquainted with the actual state of matters, and causing them to feel more thoroughly identified with us in the work. Each church has its own part to do in the cultivation of the home field, and cannot delegate its duty in this respect to another; so is it with reference to the foreign. We beg to suggest that Churches and auxiliaries, severally or conjointly, should enter into the above arrangement with one or more Mission stations, and, in addition to all the information they might otherwise receive on the subject, intercourse of this kind might prove to be beneficial in a high degree. Not that Missionaries have time for frequent and extensive correspondence, but we regard the matter in question as of great importance for their sakes, as well as for the Churches of which they are the messengers. We propose no change in the present constitution of things. It has worked well and nobly in time past, yet it cannot be denied there is too little communication in the way we desiderate. The Churches at best know us only in a general manner, and we think we are entitled to be looked upon as their representatives, not simply in name, but in reality, not merely in form, but in feeling and in fact. We allow that the Churches have enough to do with the claims and requirements of home, and may not be able to give much direct attention to foreign work. It is not necessary that they should do so. All we ask is by no means burdensome or difficult. We are persuaded there are those in every Missionary association, who would willingly undertake the task of occasional correspondents, expressive of the sympathy felt with us in our labours, and making inquiries in regard to them that would stimulate and refresh us. The result of the whole we are assured would be a more immediate and availing interest on the part of the Churches, and a deeper conviction in the case of the Missionaries, that there were many at home of a kindred spirit with us in our great and arduous enterprise.

Lastly, WE WANT MORE EARNEST PRAYER AND SUPPLICATION FOR THE OUTPOURING OF GOD'S SPIRIT UPON THE MISSIONARY WORK.

"We believe in the Holy Ghost." "He shall baptize you with the Holy Ghost and with fire." That is, with his penetrating, consuming, and all-constraining power. His influence will come down upon you from heaven with resistless might, to quicken and qualify you for my service and work. It will purify you from the evils and errors to which you are now subject, and constrain you to go forward in holy, active obedience to my will.

All this was eminently fulfilled in the history of the early Christian Church, and has been so too in the experience of numbers since that time. The same is required in the present day. We need the inspiration of the Holy Ghost for ourselves and the work in which we are engaged. We must preach the Word, which has been divinely inspired, like men into whom the same inspiration has been breathed, and Divine inspiration must be communicated to render our message effectual and apply it to the hearts and consciences of men. There can be no right work done without this heavenly inspiration,—this baptism of fire in our own case and in that of our hearers. Enkindled by it, we shall imitate the example of the noblest and most earnest of Christ's servants, and our course will be distinguished by corresponding results.

But how is this blessing to be enjoyed? By prayer. Mark the numerous promises of Scripture to this effect. Mark the command to the prophet in the valley of vision, and the vitalizing influences that attended his prayers. Mark, too, the conduct of the first apostles and disciples of the Church. "They were all with one accord in one place," and for ten days together they pleaded the promise of the Father, till the Spirit came down from on high, like a rushing mighty wind, animating and constraining them to deeds of high and holy enterprise.

This is the baptism that we want. It is indispensable that we should possess it. We pray for it ourselves. We ask the Churches to pray for it on our account. We tender this request to them. "Brethren! pray for us, that the Word of the Lord may have free course and be glorified, even as it is with you." O that this duty were more fully recognized and acted on in the case of all the followers of Christ. We are satisfied with an easy formality in the matter, a mere observance of the outward duty, while we are amazed at the seeming insuccess of our prayers, and the great disproportion between them and the answers that are received. That there is a mighty contrast apparently between the two cannot be denied. But why is it so? Have we not reason for praying as we do, and asking large things in connexion with Christ's cause and service? Has not God promised them in the fullest manner? Why then are they not in adequate measure bestowed upon us? Is it not to be found in the fact that we ask amiss,—not really or earnestly caring whether we receive the blessings that we seek,—not following up our prayers with an appropriate degree of expectation, and longing desire, and active, patient, persevering effort? We are told that we shall obtain whatever we ask in faith agreeable to the will of God,—that it shall be done for us by Christ and His Father in heaven; and it is ours to verify the promise in all manner of things. "The effectual fervent prayer of a righteous man availeth much." O that this impression were wrought into the minds and hearts of God's people and made manifest in their lives, as it respects the spread of the Gospel and the outpouring of the Holy Spirit! We are persuaded that if it were so, apart from all mystery about God's agency and man's accountability, great things would be accomplished, and the promises of Scripture would be abundantly fulfilled.

In closing, we have only to remark that we are engaged in a mighty conflict with the powers of earth and hell, but we believe in final and complete success. "We wrestle not against flesh and blood, but against the rulers of the darkness of this world, against spiritual wickedness in high places." Yet we are confident of a glorious victory. We stand in front of the frowning battlements of heathenism, but they are doomed to fall. We are surrounded by the numerous emblems of idolatry and superstition, which it is ours, under God, to overthrow. We see hundreds of millions of our fellow men in circumstances of appalling sin and evil, that are soul destroying in their character and results. This has been the case all through the ages that are past, but it is our object to set them free, and bring them to the knowledge of God and Christ, and to the enjoyment of peace and purity and eternal life. This is not our work, but God's. We are mere instruments in His hand for its accomplishment, and in connexion with all earnest and devoted labour it is ours to join in the prayer of the universal Church.

ARISE! O LORD! AND PLEAD THINE OWN CAUSE. COME FROM THE FOUR WINDS, O BREATH, AND BREATHE UPON THESE SLAIN THAT THEY MAY LIVE! THY KINGDOM COME. THY WILL BE DONE ON EARTH AS IT IS IN HEAVEN.

CHAPTER X.

MISSIONARY DISCOURSE.

"WHERE is the wise? where is the scribe? where is the disputer of this world? hath not God made foolish the wisdom of this world? For after that in the wisdom of God, the world by wisdom knew not God, it pleased God by the foolishness of preaching to save them that believe." 1 COR. i, 20, 21.

VARIOUS interpretations have been given of this passage. For the right understanding of it, we must be acquainted with the moral and spiritual condition of the old heathen world, and the bearing of Christianity that was in conflict with it at the time. Paul knew this subject well and wrote accordingly. We have here some of his profoundest views in regard to it, which are of practical and far-reaching application.

The Greeks boasted of their wisdom and philosophy, and on this account were held in high honour by the nations round about. But the apostle judged of it differently from other men. He looked at it from a Divine stand-point, and under Divine influence denounced it as vain and foolish, and he was amply sustained in this opinion by a consideration of its character and effects.

There was another thing, however, in which he gloried, and of which he was warranted to speak in the highest terms. He called it "the foolishness of preaching." Such was the estimate which others had formed of it. Such was the epithet commonly attached to it by those around him, while he firmly believed in its Divine origin, and was able to adduce satisfactory proof of its saving influence and design. It was in his view indispensably necessary from the circumstances of the case, as the only availing antidote to the evils and errors that were everywhere current in the earth.

There is no country perhaps that so much resembles ancient Greece in many respects as China at the present day. It has long boasted of, and been widely famed for, its wisdom and learning, its civilization and culture. But the more we consider these in their moral aspect and bearing, we are the more convinced of the importance and necessity of the truths which the Apostle was engaged in making known. The moral and spiritual condition of the great empire of China is practically the same as that of Greece and Rome in the times of the Apostle, and it is interesting to contemplate the subject from this point of view. We are able to understand these words and similar passages of holy writ better, by the light of an actual acquaintance with the state of things in China, than by any mere general speculation, or by the researches and discoveries of other men.

We can intensely appreciate the sentiments of the inspired writer, as he describes his own corresponding field of Missionary labour. We can enter into deepest sympathy with him, and realize from our own experience and observation, his parallel impressions of the times in which he lived, and the circumstances in which he was placed. We are thus able to read the past in large measure by the light of the present. The differences existing between the civilized East and West, in ancient and in modern times, are not so great as to prevent our seeing a wonderful similarity, and in that proportion we can estimate the necessity and advantage of the Apostle's ministry equally in the one case as in the other.

We intend to direct your thoughts to China in the consideration of our text, as a field with which we profess to be familiar, and which is calculated to shed no small degree of light upon it. Our sermon will be strictly a Missionary one, and in that respect it may be all the more peculiar. In the first place, we shall notice what the Apostle means by the wisdom of this world, and in the second place, by the foolishness of preaching.

I. The Wisdom of this world.

How shall we best determine this in the sense we have proposed? We cannot do it better perhaps than by examining the various questions contained in the text, and the statement made by the Apostle in evidence of what was implied in them.

"Where is the wise?" This term answers to a class of men who lived in China thousands of years ago. They bear such names as Yaou, Shun, Yu, Tang, Wăn, Woo, Chow-Kung, and Kung-foo-tsze. These names are in no wise suggestive to you, but in the hearing of millions of your fellow men elsewhere, they awaken the deepest response of their souls. These sages or holy men of China were distinguished for piety and moral excellence, and they are spoken of as patterns of all that was praiseworthy in personal conduct and in official life. Among them the name of Kung-foo-tsze or Confucius stands pre-eminent. He lived about five hundred years before the Christian era, and in early life sought to obtain some public post, in order to carry out his principles of moral and political reform. With the exception of a short period, however, he was disappointed, and accordingly gave himself to the education of several thousand disciples. These in time spread abroad his fame in all directions, and through their influence he has become the great venerated sage of China. Temples have been erected for his honour and worship in every city, which are visited at stated times by the highest authorities and scholars in the country, and where solemn worship and sacrifices are offered to him and his compeers in the literary pantheon. On approaching any of these temples, one observes four Chinese characters over the front gate, which mean the equal of heaven and earth. They are a quotation from the ancient classics, and denote that Confucius particularly, in respect of his wisdom and goodness, was equal to the greatness of heaven and earth; and as these are in fact the supreme divinities of China, the sage is thus placed on a level with them, while the language otherwise employed in reference to him is fully in harmony with this idea. He is spoken of as the teacher of ten thousand ages, most holy, most perfect, and without compare. On entering the temple no idols are to be seen, only a number of small wooden tablets on a graduated altar, among which that of Confucius appears foremost. It bears the inscription—"To the spirit of our sacred venerated sage Kung-footsze." There are similar inscriptions on the other tablets ranged alongside, but only a secondary kind of worship is paid to them. The Chinese think of Confucius as the embodiment and perfection of all moral goodness, and as the source of all the learning and civilization that exist in the country. They suppose themselves indebted to him on this account beyond conception, and therefore honour and revere him in the highest manner.

"Where is the scribe?" This name answers to a class of men who were the immediate followers or disciples of Confucius. They were devoted to the recording of his sayings and the compilation of his books, and the whole collection now forms the sacred standard literature of China. The subjects treated of are virtue and morality, politics and government, history and poetry, rites and ceremonies, and the universal harmony of men and things. In the twelfth century of our era, a set of philosophers commented on these various writings, and their explanations, appended to the original text by Imperial order, are equally taught in all the schools throughout the empire.

"Where is the disputer of this world?" Or rather, where is the disputant of the present age? This term denotes a class of men now living. They are the teachers or scholars of China. They are to be met with in all directions, and are looked upon with extreme respect by those around them. They are the students of the ancient classics. They belong to what is called the Confucian religion, whether they have graduated or not at the official examinations. They are the leaders of public opinion, the teachers of youth, strongly attached to the old order of things, and averse to anything like change and innovation in the established *régime* of the country. They form the controversialists of the age, and are the great opponents to all Missionary effort, as well as to all foreign enterprise in China.

"Hath not God made foolish the wisdom of this world?" Hath not God made the wisdom of this world to appear worthless and foolish? You observe that the wisdom of China is contained in the classic books called by the name of Confucius, though really he is the author of only a small portion of them. As it is, however, these books are declared to be the repository of all wisdom, human and divine, the knowledge of which has placed China high in the vantage ground, as compared with all other nations. There is no learning supposed to be equal to what is taught in these ancient writings, and great and manifold are the advantages believed to be connected with the study and understanding of them. But as Paul said of the wisdom of his day, so we may remark with equal truth of the classic wisdom of China,—"hath not God made foolish the wisdom of this world?" Why? Observe, the question amounted to a positive affirmation of its being the case. It was made in fulfilment of an ancient prophecy contained in the previous verse,—"I will destroy the wisdom of the wise and bring to nothing the understanding of the prudent." That is, I will confound the wisdom and learning of these wise men and philosophers, however much esteemed and followed they may be. The reason of this will shortly appear, only we remark that the prophecy has been wonderfully fulfilled in application to the wisdom and learning of ancient Greece and Rome. Where is their wisdom now? What is thought of it? The systems then elaborated and universally honoured have disappeared, or are looked at only as a thing of the past, exerting no influence whatever on the opinions and practices of men. History strikingly confirms the truth of these words at the present day, and the same is destined to be the case in reference to all other heathen systems in every part of the world. The wisdom of China is included in this prophecy. It has long prevailed among the millions of its votaries, and has been deemed incomparable in their view; but the sentence of condemnation has been pronounced against it, and it is as doomed to fall as the wisdom of bygone ages in the West. Our patience may be severely exercised, and we may wonder as to the time and method of its accomplishment. But we need be under no doubt in the matter. "One day is with the Lord as a thousand years, and a thousand years as one day." There was little likelihood of the civilization and culture, the learning and wisdom of Greece and Rome being overthrown in the sense here intended, but we see that such has been the case; and in so far as the wisdom of China partakes of a like character and is productive of like effects, it will cease to be in the Providence of God, and a new era will dawn in connexion with the spread and influence of our holy and Divine Christianity.

The Apostle goes on to describe the occasion of this overthrow, from the bearing and issues of the wisdom of this world, in the experience and condition of those who submitted to it or were affected by it. He says,—"For after that in the wisdom of God, the world by wisdom knew not God." What is the meaning of these words? We may paraphrase them in the following manner:—"For when in the All-wise Government and Providence of God, in the lapse of ages, the whole heathen world by reason of its wisdom and philosophy, its speculations and vain imaginings, attained this melancholy result,—that it knew not God, in other words, lost the knowledge of God." This is the idea of the text. It is not that the world failed to attain the knowledge of God by means of its wisdom and speculations, but that in very consequence of these, it lost what it originally possessed, and brought itself into a state of utter ignorance and error in regard to God and Divine things.

We have proof to this effect in two corresponding passages of the Apostle's writings. In the first chapter of his epistle to the Romans, we have these words,—"Because that when they knew God, they glorified Him not as God, neither were thankful, but became vain in their imaginations, and their foolish heart was darkened. Professing themselves to be wise, they became fools." And again,—"As they did not like to retain God in their knowledge, so God gave them over to a reprobate mind." The idea of these passages is that the heathen were primarily possessed of the knowledge of God, but they acted in such a way as to forfeit it, as practically to eradicate it from their minds, and become dispossessed of it in their lives. And this is confirmed by our text in the clearest manner. The wisdom as well as the wickedness of the heathen was the direct occasion of their losing the knowledge of God, and of rendering them "without hope and without God in the world."

All this admits of being verified in the case of the Chinese to the fullest extent. They are in a corresponding state and condition, and it has been brought about by a similar course of things.

Let us examine the State religion of China in evidence of this fact. It has been handed down from time immemorial, and the services connected with it are performed in the temple of Heaven at Pekin. When visiting it some years ago, I was impressed with the associations round about it. It is a circular building with windows of small blue pillared glass. It has two overhanging domes of yellow tiles, and is surmounted by a gilded ball. When the sun shines upon it, the appearance is very striking. It is enclosed by a wall of several miles in circumference, within which is a varied scenery of copse and level ground. The temple is reached by a series of marble steps, and the whole has a most imposing appearance. The inscription overhead is—the Temple of the Supreme Ruler, or God, in the Chinese language. Once a year the Emperor repairs to it for worship after days of solemn fasting and preparation. He seats himself for a time within the sacred temple, and when the sacrifices are brought from the neighbouring slaughter-houses, he appears in front of an immense altar, where they are presented as a whole burnt-offering to God. At a little distance there is a beautiful marble terrace, on the top of which there are three tables of the same material. The Emperor kneels in front of the central one, and presents his prayer to the Supreme Ruler, that the blessings of spring, summer, autumn and winter may descend upon him and the myriad people over whom he reigns. He is surrounded on these occasions by the highest officials, but he alone can properly engage in the service, and that too in the humblest manner, as the Being to be worshipped is so surpassingly great and glorious. No idol or image has ever been allowed in connexion with this imperial ritual or state religion, and it is to be regarded as a monument of the ancient monotheism of the empire. In different parts of the city, temples have been erected to the spirits or angels who are supposed to be engaged as the servants or messengers of the Supreme, in accordance with our own ideas of that class of beings, and to others who are supposed to preside over the general economy of nature. They are honoured in an inferior degree, and prayed to as mediators or intercessors, who are also capable of bestowing blessings upon their votaries.

Now we should expect that this ancient ritual would have tended to keep alive the idea of the existence and unity and perfections of God throughout the country. It must be confessed, however, that this is not the case. The fact is, that the service has to do with the Emperor alone, and has no connexion with the great multitude of the people. They have no part in it at all, and there is no influence arising from it, so far as they are concerned.

The ideas originally associated with it have been well nigh lost sight of, even by those who are in the habit of engaging in it. They have at least only vague and confused ideas on the subject, and observe it simply from custom and form, as an old-established national service. But we have more to say of it than this.

A class of religionists has arisen in the empire called by the name of Taouists or Rationalists, which has perverted and corrupted the ancient system of worship for their own idolatrous and superstitious purposes. They have formed a system at the head of which an idol has been placed, of corresponding name to the Supreme Ruler of the State Ritual, and under him a vast host of spirits or divinities in harmony with the spirits or angels of the old economy. This system is now universally propagated, and from the identity of its names and titles, the common people think only of it, while they have utterly forgotten the more spiritual ideas of the ancient religion. As belonging to it, we have gods of heaven and earth; gods of the sun, moon, and stars; gods of the wind and rain, thunder and lightning; gods of the mountains and valleys; gods of the rivers and seas; gods of the city and country; gods of the houses, shops and temples; gods of war, wealth, and sickness, and many other things, suited to the circumstances and wants of all classes of the people, whether living or dead. These are eagerly followed by the superstitious multitude, and the priests are in constant requisition to perform the rites and ceremonies peculiar to their worship. Thus—"the world by wisdom has lost the knowledge of God."

Again, let us examine the teachings of the ancient classics which are of such paramount importance in the country. The farther we go back in our investigation of them, we find the most distinct and positive references to the Divine Being. His existence, perfections, and moral government, are spoken of in the clearest manner; and as these books are diligently studied by the numerous scholars of China, we might suppose that in this way they would become acquainted and impressed with the great and glorious truth. But we stated some time ago, that in the twelfth century of our era, commentaries were written upon these classics, by men whose principles were thoroughly atheistic, similar to the materialists of our own day. They did away with all the allusions to the personality of God in the various books before them. They declared that the terms Supreme

Ruler were synonymous with fate, order, necessity, eternal reason, the great extreme, the primal energy, and such like phrases. The references in these books to the spirits of heaven and earth, the angels or heavenly messengers and the tutelary deities of the world, were transformed by them into the mere elements or influences of nature, which had vast power and authority, but no personal conscious existence, such as had been originally ascribed to them. These sentiments are taught in the classic commentaries which are everywhere read and studied, along with other writings of the same class, and give form and character to the opinions of all the teachers and scholars in the empire. They have received the royal sanction for seven hundred years and are the established official orthodoxy of the day. No originality or independence of thought is ever shown or exercised in the matter, and the myriads of youth that are trained in the ancient literature of their country are imbued with the atheism and materialism thus incorporated with it. These ideas are taught by rule and law. They are enforced by the highest authority in the land. They have all the potency of confirmed habit and practice, and any departure from them would be looked upon as strange, as a revolt from the universal order of things, and as pandering either to the low class idolatries around, or to the still more reviled opinions of the foreigners that have come into the country.

In this manner too—"the world by wisdom has lost the knowledge of God."

Once more, let us examine the general sentiments or convictions of the people. There is a curious compound in their minds of the ancient form of things and the later superstitions now current in China. They have certain impressions as to Divine things which seem to be a kind of natural religion, and by means of which a sympathy can be awakened within them to some extent in harmony with our ideas of things. Still these are so overgrown or buried by the circumstances in which they have been placed, that it is difficult to impart to them clear and correct views of the truth. When talking about the Creation and Government of the world, the Fatherhood of God, and the moral obligations resting upon us in consequence, it is comparatively easy to persuade them as to the fact and importance of these things. They will acquiesce in the evidences of the Divine existence and authority, the duty of worshipping Him, and the folly and uselessness of the idolatry practised in the temples. At the same time they identify God with heaven and earth, which they regard as their father and mother, to whom they are indebted for all the blessings they enjoy, and whom they ought supremely to revere and worship. They do not suppose there can be any higher or nobler existence or conceptions than those relating to these natural objects, which in their view are the first and the formers of all things. This is their ordinary style of talk. God has been merged in their estimation with the work of His hands. It is in part the fruit of the materialistic teaching in the native schools, and they rest contented with the ideas and expressions to which they have been accustomed from their earliest days. The idolatry around them is also observed in great measure from mere habit and custom. They and their ancestors have practised it in time past, and they fear the abandonment of it, not from any deep conviction as to its truth, but from the possible harm of renouncing what others have so long and so widely followed. In this point of view, their acknowledgment of the Supreme Ruler, the God of their fathers, is confined to the idol of that name in the Rationalistic Pantheon; and so familiar are they with it, while they are so ignorant of all besides, that it is hard to divest them of the notion, when we speak to them of Him who is a spirit, and who alone has a right to their honour and worship. Thus it is again that "the world by wisdom has lost the knowledge of God."

We might still further advert to the Buddhistic system, which has exerted such a wide-spread influence in China and in other places. Its essential idea is the deification of human nature. Its founder was born in India several hundred years before the Christian era, and became a priest in his early life. He gained a multitude of followers, who seemed to have been wonderfully impressed with his character and teachings. In due time he announced to them that he had become Buddha, or the enlightened one, and that he had attained the standard of perfect intelligence. He said that he could see through the system of things universally existing, and he was worshipped as God accordingly. The idea of Buddhism is that a human being is capable of advancing in the scale of intelligence and purity by a long course of transmigration, and especially by complying with its tenets, so that he may reach up to the highest point of existence. It is one of continual, and, it may be, everlasting progress. There is no conception of God in our sense attached to the theory, only man is elevated to the Divine, the sinful and depraved to the holy and perfect, the miserable and wretched to the peaceful and happy. In view of the millions who are the professed votaries of this creed in all parts of Eastern Asia, it is a matter for deep and overwhelming thought, that it should thus be devoid of the very idea of God. In reference to no other system, is the language before us so appropriate. The highest human wisdom perhaps has been at work in forming and perpetuating it. It has attained the greatest notoriety in the world. It has exerted a mighty influence for many ages and over a vast portion of the earth. It stands at the head of all religions in the number and variety of its worshippers, and yet its characteristic creed is Atheism. Its acknowledged faith is man raised by a lengthened process of purification and merit to a stage in the scale of being, in which annihilation or unconsciousness, the absence of all pain and pleasure, evil and infirmity, constitutes the crowning mark, and which is called the Buddhaship, the supreme intelligence, the divinity. Truly we may say of this system in its character, operation and effects,—"the world by wisdom has lost the knowledge of God."

Such is the condition of things in China. We are persuaded you will agree with us in regard to the language of the text. All the peculiar wisdom of that country has directly led to this result. Ungodliness is the melancholy issue of the whole. Strange that such should be the case, but we see in the fact a striking exemplification of what the Apostle saw and felt in reference to Greece and Rome in his day. The same state of things is reproduced in the East now, that he observed in the West, and the same picture must be drawn, and the same description given of the moral and spiritual condition of the four hundred millions of China, that was done of other lands in former times. The world by wisdom, that is in very consequence of its wisdom and philosophy, has lost the knowledge of God.

We now proceed to the other part of our subject. II. The Foolishness of preaching. "For when the world by wisdom knew not God, it pleased God by the foolishness of preaching to save them that believe."

Preaching—what is it? We can be at no loss on looking at the context. It is the public announcement of Christ and Him crucified, the proclaiming in the hearing of all the way of salvation through Him,—the great facts of His Person, character, and work,—His Divinity, incarnation, holy life, atoning death, resurrection and ascension, with the offer of pardon and eternal life through Him. In a word, it is the unfolding, in the fullest and freest manner, of Jesus Christ as the Son of God and the Saviour of the world. This was the idea which the Apostle had of preaching. It was his mission, and the same is the estimate that your Missionaries have formed and acted on in their department. It is the work to which they have been appointed, for which they have left their native land, and in which they have been engaged for many long years in China.

The Apostle felt he had the highest warrant and authority for his office as a preacher of the Gospel. There were those who ridiculed him in the discharge of it, as if he had neither right nor reason on his side for acting as he did. But he prosecuted his work under the noblest impulses, and in obedience to the supreme command of Him whose he was and whom he served. There was the commission which he considered it an honour and

T

privilege, as well as a most solemn duty, to fulfil. "Go and preach the Gospel to every creature." So it is with reference to your Missionaries of the present day. Many revile the work of preaching, and propose other schemes for the enlightenment and civilization of mankind. But without disparaging these in their proper place, we cannot forego the commission that has been entrusted to us. Until it is revoked, it is ours to obey it to the utmost possible extent. We believe that wisdom and authority are connected with it of the highest kind, and it were folly and disobedience to neglect or despise it, while it continues to retain all the sanctions and obligations it originally possessed.

Besides there is wonderful adaptation in the condition of China for the literal accomplishment of this Divine command. You have been informed of the prevalence of education and learning throughout the country. Not that it is at all equal to our ideas of things, but so far as it goes, it qualifies millions of the people for reading their own language and apprehending the truths we are in the habit of proclaiming amongst them. In this respect the Chinese stand high in comparison with all other heathen nations, and it is a great thing in connexion with our work to find a people thus prepared for it. We are not under the same necessity of opening schools and furnishing the elements of education that obtains in other Mission fields. The Chinese highly appreciate their own extensive literature, and schools exist in all directions for the study of it, so as to train the youth of the country for the varied business of life. All this is of great service to us, as it enables us to engage in the work of preaching in the most literal manner, as the best adapted to the condition of the people, and to distribute our Christian books with advantage, assured of their being read and understood by multitudes in every place.

But what is the extent to which preaching is carried on in China? Keep in mind here that it is not long since the country was opened to Missionary effort, and that since then much had to be done in the way of acquiring the language, and other preparatory work. Allowing this, what may be said on the subject? By the treaties of 1842 and 1860 a number of ports were opened for foreign intercourse, which were for the most part occupied by Missionaries as soon as possible. Chapels were erected at these places as our head quarters, where the Gospel has been preached from day to day, sometimes to a few and at other times to hundreds assembled to hear the Word. In the immediate thoroughfares also, we have been in the habit of preaching to large and attentive audiences. The country districts in the immediate neighbourhood have been extensively gone over, and the interior for hundreds, and in some instances for thousands of miles, has been penetrated, for the simple object of proclaiming the Gospel to the people around. The amount of work performed in this way cannot be told. Millions of the Chinese have thus heard the joyful sound, and by means of our Bible and tract distributors multitudes have received copies of our Christian books. Not a few of the Missionaries have attained to great freedom in the use of the Chinese tongue. Their aptitude in this matter is acknowledged by the natives themselves, and they have employed it largely in the work of preaching. This is the course we habitually pursue, and you can form from it some idea of the extent to which we engage in it. We need not dwell at present on the characteristics of our preaching, or the effects apparently attendant upon it. It is our aim to adapt ourselves to the requirements of the occasion, meeting the wants of those whom we address in the simplest and most intelligent manner, entering as we best can into their circumstances and condition, solving their difficulties, and employing such illustrations as shall most clearly show them the excellence and authority of the Gospel of Christ. On week days and on the Sabbath days, by free and friendly conversation, and by stated and regular service, we endeavour to communicate to one and all the message of salvation, and urge it on their individual and cordial acceptance. These labours have doubtless been followed by a wide-spread diffusion of Christian truth. Multitudes have in this way been made generally acquainted with it, preparatory to the more extensive and complete evangelization of the empire.

We go on to notice what the apostle calls the "foolishness of preaching." It is a striking phrase and hard to be understood from a ministerial point of view. Missionaries, however, are able to apprehend it, and can sympathize with Paul most fully in regard to it. Let us see how the preaching of the Gospel is stigmatized by the Chinese in this manner.

First of all, there is the foreign aspect of it. You are already aware of the pride and prejudice, the bigotry and self-conceit of the Chinese. They have the highest ideas of themselves as a nation, while they look with something like contempt and scorn upon all other people. They have a civilization and a culture which they think far superior to what are to be found elsewhere, and they are in the habit of speaking of us as only barbarians and devils. The Greeks and Romans of old in their similar estimate of outside nations have their compeers in the case of the Chinese. They have formed a low opinion of the tribes and communities round about them, and there is, undoubtedly, a great contrast between such and themselves. But they transfer these depreciating ideas to every other nation on the face of the earth, and judge of them from what they know of those in their immediate neighbourhood. It is enough that we have not been born in their country, that we have not shared in the blessings of their high and peculiar civilization, and the idea of us barbarians and foreigners coming to teach and enlighten them is preposterous enough. In a word, we know the significance of such passages in holy writ from the Chinese application of them,—"What will this babbler say?" "Can any good thing come out of Nazareth?" "These men being Jews, who have turned the world upside down, are come hither also, and teach customs which it is not lawful for us to receive, neither to observe, being Romans." Such is the estimate which the proud and high-minded scholars of China form of us and our message. It is sufficient reason in their view that we are foreigners, and that our doctrine is foreign, to vilify our work as the "foolishness of preaching."

Again, the charge is made from the negative aspect of our preaching when it is judged of from their point of view. It is not preaching or teaching that the Chinese object to, but the character of it in our case that is declared to be foolish. They have like work largely carried on among themselves, and by this means the country people have been made familiar with the teachings of their wise men, the historical events of former days, and have been converted to the faith and practice of idolatry. The point is, however, that our preaching lacks in the invariable elements of all Chinese instruction, namely—veneration for Confucius, and the duty of ancestral worship. These are adhered to with the greatest tenacity by all classes, and no innovation has ever been allowed to interfere with them or weaken their influence in the minds and observances of the people. Christianity comes into conflict with them, and is specially opposed on this ground. It is charged with intolerance. Other religions such as the Buddhist and Taouist will allow these national services to the utmost. They are accommodated to them and render them subservient to their own idolatrous and superstitious purposes, but it is not so with the doctrine of Jesus, and on this account it is charged with foolishness. Nothing is more reasonable or becoming in the opinion of a Chinaman than the worship of the sages and the ancestors, and it is enough to stamp Christianity with absurdity from its not allowing anything of the kind. Our converts are reproached on this single ground, as if they were guilty of neglecting and dishonouring the dead, whom it was their duty to revere, and whose happiness and existence in the other world are so intimately connected with the services and sacrifices of posterity on earth.

Once more, the charge is brought against our preaching from the positive elements that are contained in it. These are, in the main, the sin and depravity, the ruin and helplessness of human nature on the one hand, and the Divine Person and atoning work of our Lord Jesus Christ on the other. With regard to the former, the Chinese hold that man is born radically good, and if he allows subordinate principles and other evil influences to gain the advantage over him, he is certainly to be blamed, but it is in his power to remedy the evil and to return to his original integrity. Various means have been devised for this purpose in connexion with the different systems in operation in the country. With regard to the latter, it has no correspondence in the religious views and observances of the Chinese. Their worship and sacrifices to heaven and earth, the sages, the ancestors, and the idols in the temples, are not of an expiatory or atoning character at all. They are simply in the way of thank-offering and supplication, and the Chinese have no conception of the worth or necessity of such a propitiation as Christianity provides for our fallen race. On both grounds, therefore, our preaching is charged with foolishness, marked as it is by these fundamental elements, and always insisting as it does on their being indispensable points of the Christian faith. Christ and Him crucified are specially an occasion of ridicule and scorn on the part of the scholars and teachers of China. They will commend our exhortations on all moral subjects, lamenting with ourselves the vice and the evil that are everywhere current. They will coincide with us in all our preaching on natural theology, the Being, perfections, government and providence of God, His mercy and goodness, the duty of Divine worship, the necessity of repentance, and the certainty and solemnity of a judgment day. No objection is ever tendered to what we have to say on these momentous themes, but when Christ and the Cross, Jesus and the Resurrection are brought before them, the old stigma is levelled against us. Many a time have I been in these circumstances, encouraged by the attention and interest of a number of intelligent looking men to what I was advancing on the ordinary topics of morality and natural religion, but when the final declaration was made about Christ and His salvation, and pressed upon their acceptance, their contempt and scorn became manifest, and they turned away sneering alike at His blessed name, His messenger, and His message.

What then? Is this all? No, happily. "It pleased God by the foolishness of preaching to save them that believe."

Believe in what? In the foolishness of preaching, that is, in spite of the stigma and the scorn attached to it. Need we say here that it is an easy thing for you to believe in Christ in this Christian land. You are surrounded by influences all tending to this result, and I might observe in the circumstances that it is almost easier for you to believe in Him than not. You have a positive resistance to make in order to continue in a state of unbelief and practical rejection of the truth. But it is wholly otherwise in China. All the influences at work there are on the opposite side.

People are called to believe what seems to every one to be "the foolishness of preaching," and a hundred adverse ideas cluster around the expression, which are to be understood and realized only by those whom they directly concern. Be this as it may, there are those who believe in China, as there were such in the days of Paul, notwithstanding the peculiarity and peril of doing so. Writing to the same Corinthian church, he says, "Now thanks be unto God, who always causeth us to triumph in Christ, and maketh manifest the savour of His knowledge by us in every place." As Missionaries to China, we can sympathize with the Apostle in these glowing and grateful words. There are those who believe in that part of the world in spite of all the difficulties and dangers connected with it. Though not regarding statistics as if they determined the full value and bearing of Mission work, yet it is encouraging to be able to adduce them to some extent. When I went to China about twenty years ago, there were not more converts than would fill three or four seats of an ordinary English chapel. Now there are as many as would require five such places of worship, or one equal to Mr. Spurgeon's tabernacle, to contain them. In the former case there were hardly twenty individuals, and now there are nearly six thousand in all. Many more, however, than even these have been in fellowship with us, but death, political troubles, and other causes have been at work in reducing the list, still we contemplate the success thus reaped with thankful hearts. We are compelled to say of it in reflecting upon the past—"What hath the Lord wrought." The Missionaries in the field have been so few, the time occupied has been so brief, and the difficulties to be overcome have been so great, that we see no reason for discouragement in these apparent results of our labours. In the circumstances, they are highly gratifying, and the more so as we believe that the work in future will be carried on more efficiently, and, with God's blessing, will be more prosperous than in its early stage.

But the question may be asked what as to the character and standing of our native converts? We answer again in the language of Paul,—"it pleased God by the foolishness of preaching to save them that believe." Such was the effect of faith in the estimation of the Apostle. It saved. And what is the meaning of the term? What is the bearing and force of it in the case of them that believe in China? In a Scriptural point of view, salvation means the forgiveness of sins, the sanctification of the heart and life, and the expectation or hope of heaven. These we know come to us through faith in Christ, and this is the ground on which our Chinese converts look for such Divine blessings in common with ourselves. Once they had no thought of them at all, now they readily acknowledge Christ to be the single object of their faith and the alone foundation of their hopes. Once they were the followers of Confucius and the other sages of their country, the slaves of idolatry and superstition, and the victims of all the evils and errors characteristic of natural depravity and heathenism. Now they have professedly renounced these, and are manifestly undergoing in numerous instances a course of moral and spiritual improvement and enlightenment, which has Christ for its model and His holy Spirit as its animating agent. We do not boast unduly of what has taken place in the experience and habits of our Christian converts, only in so far as the reality and effects of their faith are concerned, we are satisfied in the case of many of them, that they adduce all the evidence we could possibly expect at their hands, and we should not hesitate to place them on an equality with our generally approved fellow Christians at home. They are exposed to many and peculiar temptations. They are subject to various infirmities, and we are not without occasion for anxiety and sorrow on account of some of them, but this is no more than what obtains in far more favourable circumstances among ourselves.

Still without claiming the attribute of perfection for these converted men and women, which certain of our countrymen seem to demand, forgetful of their own imperfect conduct and character by the way, we are free to state as it regards all the elements of Christian life, many of them show the Gospel to be the power of God unto salvation. They are what they are, only by Divine grace, and as we look at our Christian churches in China, and note the past history and present standing of those connected with them, we are led to say—"Such were some of you, but ye are washed and justified and sanctified, in the name of the Lord Jesus and by the Spirit of our God." Their piety, their purity, their knowledge and appreciation of Divine things, are in striking contrast to what they once were. As private members of the Church, or as teachers, preachers, and ordained pastors in some instances, we thank God for the course of consistency which many of them display, while it is our earnest aim and prayer that they may be advanced in all Christian excellence, and be unceasingly prepared for serving God on earth and enjoying His favour in heaven.

And all this we admit to be in the language of the Apostle through the good pleasure of Him whose servants we are. "It pleased God by the foolishness of preaching to save them that believe." "Not unto us, O Lord, not unto us, but unto Thy name be the praise." When Dr. Morrison, the first Protestant Missionary to China, was leaving the shores of America, he was asked if he thought it possible for him to convert the Chinese, his answer was no, but he believed that God would. And we observe that this is being done in the present day. Every sinner converted, every soul saved, is so only through the gracious power of God. To Him alone be the glory; and while we bless Him for what He has accomplished of His promise hitherto, we pray that it may be the case a hundred and a thousand fold more in days to come, until all that is implied in the ancient prophecy shall be fulfilled. "Behold, these shall come from far, and lo, these from the north and from the west, and these from the land of Sinim."

In conclusion, notice the bearing and effects of all heathen philosophy.

It is Godless in its character and influence. Whatever else it may possess, it lacks one fundamental element which alone entitles it to the name of true wisdom. It is "without God." A few ancient heathen writers speculated about Divine things, and they have been much spoken of in consequence, but at the best their dissertations were exceedingly vague, uncertain, and confused. They were in utter mazes lost, except in so far as they traced their way back to the original ideas entertained as to the being, unity and perfections of God. In China this has most clearly been the case. The earliest notions on the subject were remarkably distinct and positive. They were doubtless a relic of the first revelation, but as time rolled on they were forgotten and grievously departed from. Man is unable to find out God, and his very wisdom and philosophy are in general the direct occasion of greater ignorance and error than before. Such has been the fact in ancient and modern times. A new discovery is needed of the all-important truth. Atheism and idolatry, spiritualism and materialism are the order of things now as they were in former days, as much in China as they were in Greece and Rome. The religious idea has been developed, but altogether in the wrong way, and we see what is the nature and tendency of it when man is left to his own unaided efforts. His utmost wisdom when unsanctified by the Spirit of God, only leads him farther astray, and conducts to the melancholy issue described in the text. It is of no use to deny it theoretically. We appeal to facts. China and India confront the student of history and philosophy, and show in the clearest manner that the knowledge of God is to be retained and recovered, not by any mere human means, but by direct Divine teaching. It is easy to talk of man's natural instincts and powers in this Christian land, but we see them in their naked character and results in those countries that have not been favoured with the light of revelation. There the testimony is uniformly the same. The scepticism of the scholars and the superstition of the common people act and re-act upon each other, and materially increase the alienation of one and all from God and godliness.

Notice further the alone and sovereign efficacy of the Gospel.

The text is remarkable in this respect. It speaks of the intervention of the plan of mercy when man was utterly lost and ruined. He had been left for ages to himself, and every available means had been tried by him in the way of self-recovery and salvation, but in vain. Then it pleased God to appoint another instrumentality, and apply it with salutary power and effect. It was derided and opposed on all hands by the very persons it came to bless, but in God's own sovereign grace there were many who believed it unto eternal life. So is it in China at the present day. The same experiment has been repeated, and the same consequences have followed. When all human agency has failed in attaining the end in view, Christianity has come in and proved itself to be the power and wisdom of God unto salvation. It has met with manifold forms of opposition and trial, and its progress has been slow and limited from various causes, but its Divine origin and application have been verified in the most satisfactory manner. It has overcome the natural enmity of the human heart,—it has eradicated the pride and prejudice of the native mind,—it has dispelled the ignorance and error that long prevailed among those who have received it,—it has raised them in the scale of intelligence and moral being,—it has taught and trained them to worship the only true and living God, and to believe in Jesus Christ whom He hath sent,—it hath made them partakers of eternal life, in its purity, joy and hope;—and all this we ascribe to the grace, the good pleasure of its Divine Author, who commanded to make it known, and promised to bless its announcement to the ends of the earth.

Lastly, notice the necessity and importance of continued and more extended Missionary labour.

This we confess to be our only hope in reference to China. We hail every other means of enlightening and civilizing the nation, allowing them to be directed and sanctified by Christian influence. They are needful in their place. They will help to break down the reserve and exclusiveness of the Chinese, and open the way for a freer and fuller development of Gospel truth. But we maintain that it is that truth in its simplicity, in its purity, and in its power, which is the panacea for all the evils and errors of the country. China needs to be, and can only be regenerated by the Gospel of the Grace of God in Christ Jesus. It requires to be made known by men qualified for the purpose, animated and constrained by the holiest motive and under Divine inspiration, who will go everywhere preaching the message of salvation like the apostles and evangelists of early days. We want men of this class and character to enlist for the work. "Whom shall I send, and who will go for us," are words that indicate God's will in the matter. Or in clearer and more emphatic terms still, we have the commission of our Lord to His disciples—" Go and preach the Gospel to every creature." What is the answer tendered to these thrilling words on the part of those now hearing me? Are there any of you ready to say in the fulness and fervour of your souls—"Lord, here am I, send me!" Seek His gracious direction in regard to it. Ask His same self-consecrating spirit to rest upon you. And if called to engage in this blessed work and preach the Gospel in the great realms of heathendom, it will be yours to be identified with Him in this highest and noblest enterprise, and to share in the glorious issues that are connected with it.

Brethren! We want more men and means for carrying on the Missionary cause in China. We want the united interest, sympathy, efforts, and prayers of the whole Christian Church in the undertaking. We want the Gospel to be preached effectually and with power over the length and breadth of the land, as the divinely appointed means of its enlightenment, conversion and salvation. We appeal to you on the subject. We ask your co-operation in the work, and when the promise regarding it is fulfilled, you shall participate in the joy of the Saviour and in the thanksgivings of the saved. Amen.

APPENDIX.

We append the following remarks in order to meet various inquiries that have been made on certain topics referred to in the preceding pages, but which admit of fuller illustration.

I. THE DIVINE NAME.

We have assumed that the terms *Shang-te*, or Supreme Ruler, express in Chinese the name of God. There is the idea of Majesty or Power connected with them which is natural and appropriate, and answers to the nomenclature employed in many other languages, alike ancient and modern. The Chinese consider that earth is in a measure the counterpart of heaven, and the Emperor or Imperial Ruler in the one case corresponds in title and position, though in an infinitely lower degree, to the Supreme Ruler in the other. The Imperial name, *Hwang-te*, denotes in Chinese the highest authority on earth, and the Supreme name, *Shang-te*, similarly denotes the highest authority in heaven. Though there has been grievous perversion in this matter from the coming in of the Taouist idolatry, yet even there the same ideas obtain, and the same phraseology is made use of. At all events, the ancient monotheistic sentiments are confirmed by the names respectively given to God in heaven, and His vicegerent on earth. We have alluded to the term Heaven as applied to the Divine Being, from His throne being in heaven, and of whom it is an emphatic emblem. In the same way the Emperor of China is commonly spoken of as the Son of Heaven, to express his official relationship to the Supreme Ruler; and the court, or palace, or throne, are words frequently used in reference to him, so as to avoid a careless mention of the name or title of His Imperial Majesty.

The terms for God in the Chinese language have the most direct and personal significance. There is no resemblance in this respect to the pantheistic system of India. The acts and attributes ascribed to the Supreme Ruler in the ancient classics are as much of a personal nature, as those that are done or possessed by the Imperial Ruler on earth. It has been mentioned by some that the materialism of after days has altered the original bearing of the name, or of its correlative—Heaven, and has rendered both unsuitable in a Christian point of view. It was this that induced the Roman Catholics to adopt another term by Papal command, namely, the Lord of Heaven. This certainly gives the idea of personality at once, but it has just the same meaning that is implied in the original designation, *Shang-te*, which has the further advantage of being thoroughly Chinese, and more suggestive of Supreme Majesty than the other. We can readily graft ideas upon it that are in perfect harmony with its most obvious import, with its acknowledged application in the ancient classics, and with the natural sentiments of the people at large. By means of it, in connection with our Christian teaching, we hope to obviate the perverted and idolatrous use that has been made of the phrase, and impart to the Chinese, in a purer form, the knowledge of the God of their fathers that has been lost among them for many ages.

II. THE CHRONOLOGY OF CHINA.

We do not claim for the Chinese any very high or peculiar antiquity. There is nothing in their history, language, or civilization that requires us to do so. The more these are examined, we are persuaded that they have existed as a nation within a period that may easily be allowed. The thing which makes them stand out in such a striking manner from other people is their continuity and preservation from early times. Other countries or kingdoms that were contemporaneous with them have disappeared, while they have maintained their individuality without any remarkable change, and gone on apparently increasing in prosperity and power. It is asserted by some that the farther we go back in the investigation of their history, language, political and social condition, we are compelled to acknowledge a much greater antiquity regarding them than is generally admitted. Distinguished names are on the side of this theory, but it is in our view unsupported by facts, and it is not required by the necessities of the case. The rise and progress of many countries in modern times might be adduced in evidence of the probability of the Chinese becoming what they are now, or having been what they were formerly, without allowing any very extraordinary age on their part. As to other Asiatic nations, the most ancient of the Hindoos, for example, we have no difficulty in admitting an equal, or even a greater antiquity to them, than what we are disposed to do in regard to the Chinese.

The *onus* of proving or denying a long chronology in their case, we leave to those who are conversant with that class of people. There may or may not be a basis for it in the traces of an advanced civilization among them, or in the structure of their well-formed and inflected language. It appears to us, however, that no argument of this kind can be drawn from China. Their civilization is indeed peculiar, but not so striking as to require a greater period than we have asked for its commencement and spread. The first fathers of the people, as they entered the country, were comparatively few, and for many generations they were confined to a limited portion of what now constitutes the whole empire. It seems, too, that at the outset, they were possessed of considerable knowledge on various subjects, fitting them for the direction and control of the colony then established. They brought with them elements of information that were soon turned to objects of practical utility, which we observe to exist amongst them at the present day. Their separation from the main body of the human species, or from other branches of it, is in no wise surprising to us, when we consider its character and effects. We are not acquainted with the events or incidents that then occurred, but a sufficient amount of time is allowed by us for the existence of the Chinese as a distinct people, to harmonize perfectly with the higher chronology of the Bible, and the facts of the case, as we find them in their own history and condition.

The argument from language may be alleged in support of a

more ancient date. We merely observe here, such is our opinion of it, that less can be said on this ground in relation to China than in relation to many other countries. The difficulty of accounting for the formation of various agglutinated languages, within a moderate period, is far greater in India, for instance, than it is in the case of the Chinese, which is distinguished by a naturalness and simplicity all its own. The time required for its formation, considered from our standpoint, does not appear to us necessarily long. Man was not launched into the world, or scattered over its surface, without the means of communication to a satisfactory extent, and the essential sameness of the Chinese language in its earliest records, with what is now current, suggests to us an idea of its origin, in which time is no material qualification whatever. We see the powerful influence of literature in modifying or perpetuating a spoken tongue, and the more it is cultivated and read, correspondingly great are the effects it produces on the minds and intercourse of a people. This has been wonderfully the case in China, and without it, we cannot say what deviations would have taken place in the common language of the country. At the same time, there is in general a great interaction between the two, and it is surprising how much the written and spoken forms affect and mould one another. Perhaps China is an anomaly in this respect, from the ancient classics being always made the basis of study, and the model of style, in the literary world. As bearing, however, on the age of the nation, it were easy to show that the earliest writings of China were constructed in the simplest, tersest manner, suited indeed to convey the sentiments intended, but not more cultivated and refined than the fact of a primitive period would imply. Recondite and difficult of explanation as these ancient writings sometimes are, this arises not from their rhetorical or figurative style, indicative of a high stage of cultivation, or the result of a prolonged course of study, but from the brevity of the phrases, the paucity of the words employed, as well as the uncertainty of the allusions that are contained in them. There are the bones of the language preserved to us in these ancient memorials, and it required the lapse of ages before the whole was clothed with the flesh and sinew that now appear in the literature of the day. We have no hesitation in saying that the Chinese language as used in ancient and modern times, has no occasion for a very high antiquity being attached to it, such as certain speculatists in the West seem to imagine. Judging of its formation, and in view of our ideas of the origin of language, we consider that the allowance of 2000 years before Christ is ample time for the introduction of the Chinese into the country. Their language was then such as they received it from the first fathers of the race, and it has undergone no essential change from the peculiar circumstances in which they have been placed.

We might allude to other matters in reference to the chronology of the Chinese. Superficial examiners of the ancient books have imitated the native scholars in taking everything for granted in connexion with them. Dates and other particulars have been assumed as correct, or nearly so, it being supposed as perhaps beyond our powers to verify or deny them. The more recent investigations, however, prove beyond a doubt that the dates in question are in many instances fallacious. They bear evidence of later hands, or a total disregard of truth on the part of those who recorded them. There is utter confusion on numerous points arising from this source, and we may either impeach the men on whose authority these dates are given, or suppose they were as ignorant on the subject as we ourselves may be expected to be. The result is that there is no warrant in the Chinese dates, or in the events of Chinese history, to maintain the antiquity of the Chinese people, beyond the period maintained in the Bible, when the earth was divided, and the bounds of human habitation were determined.

III. The Analogy of Language.

Much uncertainty prevails as to the form and structure of the Chinese language. It has been looked upon as a peculiar and separate tongue, unlike all other languages, and containing difficulties well nigh insurmountable. Views, however, are beginning to be entertained about it that serve to modify these ideas, and substantiate the claims of the unity of language, and of the human race all over the world.

We have stated that the Chinese has no alphabetical basis or inflectional forms. Each word stands alone, and is complete in itself. No change ever takes place in the words that compose the language. No agglutination exists in it, such as obtains in all other known tongues. Affixes and prefixes in the different parts of speech, consisting of modifications of other, and it may be, obsolete words, and intended to affect the meaning of the word in question, have no place in Chinese. There the characters are always and altogether perfect, capable of being used in connection, without the slightest alteration, but determining the meaning in that connection, as fully and as clearly as if they were agglutinated, and formed an essential part of the primary word in the sentence. The Chinese is thus identical in its construction, as also in many of its roots, with what are found in an agglutinated form elsewhere. Its analogy in the latter respect has been amply shown ; and we are persuaded that the more it is compared with the various Semitic, Aryan, and especially the Turanian tongues, its similarity will be made the more apparent. Beyond this, however, there is in the construction of Chinese a further proof of its interest and share in comparative philology. It has as distinct and definite a system of combination of words and sentences as is to be found in the grammar of any other language. Our own English tongue furnishes, perhaps, a better idea of the resemblance than any nearer one. There are fewer changes in the radical portion of the different parts of speech in it, than in most other European or Asiatic tongues, and besides the variations in tense and declination are expressed by separate particles, which, in these tongues, are shown rather by a change in the structure of the leading words. Now this state of things is perfect in Chinese. Its monosyllabic terms admit of being used unchanged, in conjunction or apposition, and are fitted to convey the idea intended with as much force and precision as in an agglutinated or inflected speech. There is no more uncertainty as to the use of different particles in the one case than in the other. These adjuncts or particles forming always complete words, with a distinct and individual meaning, have their use and meaning determined by the position which they occupy. Hence it is that a word is often changed into a noun, verb, or adjective, according to its relative bearing in connection.

It will be seen from this, that the Chinese language has nothing of the composite aspect of an inflected or agglutinated tongue. It may be easy or difficult to find out the root of a word in a tongue of that kind, and to trace its history from ancient times. Philologists take great interest in this, and it is helpful in discovering the original meaning of a word, and the changes that have occurred in it. The study is important, too, on a higher ground. The relation of ancient languages to those now employed in the country is a point of extreme value, as determining dates, events in history, and the advancing or retrograding civilization of a people. In Chinese, however, we have a fixity and oneness that are altogether peculiar. We might almost say that remoteness and nearness in its case show no difference. The language is always radically and essentially the same. There is a possibility, indeed, of tracing back the usages attached to a particular word or phrase in ancient times. Certain circumstances may have determined its adoption, or associations may cluster round it in history, which add to our interest in regard to it. But that has nothing to do with the principles of the language,—its fundamental structure, or its syntactical arrangement, which, with all its peculiarities, no more separate it from the general family of languages, than the physical, intellectual, and moral characteristics of the nation do so from those of other people. The contrariety existing between the various agglutinated or inflected languages and Chinese is more apparent than real. There is positively as much combination in the one as in the other, and this by the necessity of the case, for in that way only could the language be carried on as a medium of communication. The unchangeableness of the Chinese, or the absence of inflections, is rendered easily possible by its brief monosyllabic forms, and yet it is constructed in such a manner as to furnish an argument in the view of those acquainted with it, in behalf of its essential unity with all other known tongues, however dissimilar they may seem to be.

IV. THE CHARACTER AND INFLUENCE OF CONFUCIUS.

It is needful that this should be clearly understood, so as to arrive at a right estimate of the political and moral condition of

China. We have alluded to it in various connexions. The more we consider it, however, its importance increases in our view. Confucius is the greatest sage of China, from his being the last in the series, and from the work he is said to have done in compiling the writings of more ancient times, which, together with his own books and instructions, are everywhere read and studied. The sages who preceded him are supposed to have had many advantages on their side, which rendered it a comparatively easy thing for them to attain that position. But it was not so with Confucius. He was in humble circumstances, despised and rejected by the princes of his day, at whose hands he sought to obtain public office in vain. His disciples were the means of proclaiming his fame, though this did not occur till long after his death. For some two thousand years he has been supreme in the estimation of the Chinese, and he is regarded as the embodiment of all moral excellence, through whose teachings the nation has become what it is.

On a careful consideration of his character and doings, what appears to us to be the facts of the case? We allow that his influence is paramount in the empire. All the Chinese glory in being called his disciples, and it is supposed by many that if he had not been a great and good man, he never could have risen to his present height, or maintained it for the length of time he has actually done. We are far from agreeing with this statement in the manner in which it is often made. Confucius is to be judged by what we know of him, and the impression that he has produced on the mind and manners of China. The mere extent of his influence is no element in the calculation of its worth. Its moral value and bearing must be clearly determined.

Looking then at the history, writings, and teachings of the sage, there do not appear to us, in connexion with them, the elements, the characteristics of a very great, wise, good, and holy man. We are struck in perusing his books, or the conversations attributed to him by his immediate followers, with the utter absence of what seems to us necessary in this respect. First of all, he did not aim at or profess anything new or original in his instructions. He claimed to be a transmitter merely of the system of the ancients. He was strong on this point, and it has gained for him no small measure of celebrity. He was attached to the rites and ceremonies, the men and things of former days, and he shows this often in a very pedantic way, while he enjoins conformity to them as the *ne plus ultra* of human life and manners. He has adopted from these more ancient sages certain principles of morality and government, which have been magnified in the hands of his disciples, and made out to be profound theorems of the greatest practical importance. In his intercourse with those around him, he once and again betrays indications of littleness or meanness, and even of equivocation and untruthfulness, which lower him immensely according to our standard of what is right. His replies are sometimes evasive and dishonest in matters which he did not really know, but which it would have been honourable in him to have declared accordingly. His own writings are untrustworthy in not a few points, as if he had been careless in their composition, and this to an extent that has confounded the students of after times. The most grievous charge we bring against him, however, is his irreligious spirit. He falls far beneath the ancient sages in this respect. In their records and conduct, we observe a high degree of piety and reverence for Divine things. God is acknowledged and worshipped in the most solemn manner. But as we approach Confucius, a great and mournful change appears. The name of God is not even mentioned by him. Heaven alone is spoken of, and in a way which shows that religion was a subject in which he felt little interest or concern. His was a system of secularism, pure and simple, and he sought to inculcate it alone on the minds of his disciples, and through them on the Chinese at large.

The effect of all this we need not say has been of a vitiating and depraving kind. Allowing that the principles of virtue and morality have obtained the sanction of Confucius, and in this case have exerted a beneficial influence in the country, the example of the sage himself has been in many respects for evil. Though his evident shortcomings are defended by his votaries, and construed in a totally different light from their reality, it cannot be denied that the moral character and secularism of Confucius have had an injurious effect upon the Chinese from age to age. Not only is he wanting in the elements of true greatness, and not only is his system defective in relation to spiritual and Divine things, but both his precepts and his practices are chargeable with results, that show their nature and operation in the untruthfulness and ungodliness of the Chinese. Though he is not responsible for all the aberrations and inconsistencies of his followers, who yet boast of their adhesion to him, still we hesitate not to say that his life and the lessons connected with it have produced a baneful influence on the whole nation, and made it the peculiar, stereotyped, unprincipled nation it largely is. We are persuaded that Dr. Legge in his annotations upon the Chinese classics will fully endorse these opinions, and we take this opportunity of recording our high appreciation of his work. It is one of vast importance as unfolding the sources of Chinese culture and civilization, and his translations, with the valuable prolegomena attached to them, are calculated to be of great service to the Missionary cause.

We have only to remark further that the aggrandisement of Confucius is not the result of any personal claim that he raised during his life. It is altogether the work of his disciples, and their marvellous success is to be accounted for probably by the absence of any competitor. Confucius has been without a rival in the estimation of the Chinese all through the ages, and the whole nation has united in adding to his fame and honour. We observe in the case of the Chinese the wide-spread and enduring issues of moral influence, and how necessary it is that such influence should always be of the right kind, in the direction of what is noble and good, heavenly and Divine. As it is, the personal character and teachings of China's greatest sage, like those of "dead yet scept'red sovereigns, who rule our spirits from their urns," have moulded the history and condition of unnumbered millions, in the most solemn and affecting sense, for time and for eternity.

V. The Political State and Prospects of China.

There have been many rebellions and revolutions in the country, which might have been expected to alter in some measure the course and constitution of things. Such, however, has not been the case. Whether these rebellions came from without or from within, at the close there invariably followed a resumption of the old *régime*. The vanquished thus overcame the victors. This was owing to the firm and solidified civilization that had long prevailed in China, and to its superiority to that of the conquerors. These had no battle to fight with the maxims of the ancient sages, which seemed equally capable of observance, however much external circumstances were changed. Hence the monotony and sameness of China in all ages.

Of late years, however, matters have assumed a different appearance. The influences brought to bear on China at the hands of foreigners are new and wonderful. Western ideas do not admit of conformity or submission to the "old custom" of the country. They are revolutionary in their character and tendency. Their very presence is subversive of the ancient order of things. It cannot be otherwise. The one is totally opposed to the other, and a conflict must necessarily ensue. We have faith in the civilization of the West to this extent, and are prepared for the struggle consequent upon it, between light and darkness, truth and error, progress and development on the one hand, and conservatism and exclusiveness on the other, life and death in the social and political aspect of the people. We may endeavour to stave off the inevitable result. Some may propose measures of peace and amity, which others maintain to be on terms inconsistent with our national character and obligations. The Chinese Government may be denounced as incapable of apprehending its duty in the matter, and our own may be regarded as too vacillating and pliant, and as unfaithful to itself and its subjects from a temporizing, yielding policy. We say nothing of either side, interested though we are in the course of events and in their ultimate issue. We take our stand on the highest ground and look at China as at present in a transition state. It is beginning to feel our influence in many and various ways, and is seeking to withstand it to the utmost possible extent. We are not surprised at this. Its very opposition, however, is hopeful in our view. The greatest darkness precedes the early dawn. There is a premonition in the minds of the ruling classes, that everything connected with us is fraught with change and innovation, if not with the actual usurpation of power and authority. They dread and hate us accordingly, and are providing for their safety, as they suppose, by keeping us at a distance.

Though mistaken in one sense, they are not in another. Still they may do what they like. China is destined to bend under the overwhelming flood of Western ideas. It cannot long resist the forces to which it is now subject, and whether these are allowed to operate in a secret and silent manner, or as the consequence of strong and aggressive measures, they will be no less effectual in the end. Our various political and mercantile agencies are ordained, in the providence of God, for the enlightenment and improvement of the country. Their persistent application will not fail of success, though baffled for a time by the peculiar prejudices of the ruling powers. Already they have produced a wide-spread impression, and they need only to be continued in order that China may share in all the advantages common to our line of things.

Our hope of China is only in this direction. There is no prospect or possibility of improvement from within. It has done its utmost in the way of self-development, and we see what the nation is after long ages of trial. It has in our view reached its greatest limit, so far as any power of its own is concerned. We believe indeed in the capacity of its people for indefinite progress in the arts and elements of civilized life, but they must be aided and stimulated by us. Hence we sustain a grave and solemn responsibility. Our conduct in the matter, in harmony with our varied duties and obligations as a Christian community, would lead to many beneficial results in the moral, political, and social condition of China. It would undoubtedly bear down much of the native opposition towards us, while we could plead from it with reason and force for still greater facilities, and larger openings into the country. Though the present aspect of affairs appears to be more exclusive and hostile than ever, we believe it is only temporary. By one means or another it will be overcome, and a more liberal policy will be entered on. Let us act our part rightly in relation to China, so as to encourage it to look upon us with a friendly eye, and receive at our hands the benefits of an enlightened and advanced civilization.

VI. THE CHRISTIANIZATION OF CHINA.

Is this possible? Is it probable? There is nothing in the nature of things, in the condition and capacity of the people, in the history of the past, or in the prospects of the future, to forbid it. Changes have taken place in the religious faith of the Chinese as in that of our own country, which might lead us to hope that their conversion to the Christian faith is not unreasonable. If our faith is true, it is Divine, and as such it is adapted to the intellectual and moral wants of the Chinese, no less than to ours. In the onward progress of the race, we may fairly expect that the great enlightening and civilizing faith of the world will exert its appropriate influence in the East as it has done in the West. Events are occurring that lead us to anticipate this result. The fulness of time is hastening on, and China must open its gates to the moulding and purifying operation of our Divine Christianity.

But is it certain that such will be the case? Our ideas on this matter are founded on the text-book of our religion. We have no sure warrant on the subject apart from it. Were it not for its commands and promises, we should withhold altogether. In the light of it, however, we have no misgivings as to the future. Whatever may be comprised in the revelations of Scripture on the point, we have sufficient reason for expecting great things in connexion with the spread of the Gospel. This is all we have to do with. We ask nothing more, and in view of it we are satisfied to go on in our work, barring all apparent discouragements and trials. We believe that the various changes taking place in our intercourse with China are designed specially to promote the rise and progress of Christianity, and the overthrow of the old-established order of things. Not that these changes are necessary for our object, but they are made and are mainly subservient to it. As for the Missionaries, it is theirs to be witnesses for Christ in this great heathen land, and to follow out their end and aim by a holy, apostolic, Christ-like life and ministry. Be the difficulties what they may, be the time of China's conversion as distant as it may, these are of no concern to us. The issue is revealed as absolutely certain, and we regard it as a high honour and privilege to aid in its accomplishment. It will form a new era in the history and condition of China.

Is it asked what in that case may be the effect of Christianity upon a people that have been so long separated from the community of the race, and marked by elements and characteristics so peculiarly their own ? We answer, that they will be distinguished in many respects from what has obtained among them under the spell of their former systems. These have had a withering, deteriorating, deadening influence upon them. Notwithstanding this, there are various elements of greatness, extension, and endurance connected with them, which are destined to be strengthened, purified, and perpetuated under the reign of Heaven—the economy of Grace. Then the position and rank of China among the nations will be in no wise diminished, and it will exert a mighty determining power in their overthrow of idolatry and superstition, and in their conversion to the faith of the Gospel.

However this result may be brought about, whether by the direct exercise of imperial authority, or by the growing enlightenment of the people, we look forward to it as a glorious fact in the history of Christianity. We stand in no doubt of it whatever. It is a sure word of prophecy, and we anticipate its fulfilment as a time of universal blessing. The light and life and peace and purity of Divine Truth are to be dispensed all around. China is included in the promise of the world's regeneration, and that by means of the spread and the power of the Gospel. The sentiment of one of its scholars, as expressed to the writer, is certain of final accomplishment in regard to it. "The Cross," he said, "points in all directions, North and South, East and West, implying that its object is to extend far and wide, and that its influence is to be commensurate with the ends of the earth." The express language of Christ Himself is,—"And I, if I be lifted up from the earth, will draw all men unto Me."

List of Protestant Missions in China, and the number of Missionaries connected with them.

ENGLISH.

London Mission	19
Church	14
Wesleyan	12
English Presbyterian	10
New Connexion	4
Baptist	1
United Methodist	2
United Presbyterian	1
Irish Presbyterian	2
China Inland	21
Union Chapel	2
Independent Baptist	1
British and Foreign Bible Society	2
National Bible Society of Scotland	2
	93

AMERICAN.

American Board	18
Presbyterian	25
Protestant Episcopal	4
Southern Baptist	4
American Baptist	6
Methodist Episcopal	8
Southern Methodist Episcopal	2
United Presbyterian	2
Southern Presbyterian	4
Independent	1
Independent Baptist	1
Woman's Mission	3
	78

GERMAN AND SWISS.

Basel Mission	6
Berlin ,,	4
Berlin Ladies	4
Rhenish	4
	18

Total	189

Ordained Missionaries	143	
Lay ,,	23	
Female ,,	23	189

NORWICH: PRINTED BY FLETCHER AND SON.

MISSIONS TO CHINA.

I.
Crown 8vo, 6s. cloth, with Portrait.

A MEMOIR OF THE LATE REV. WILLIAM C. BURNS, M.A., Missionary to China. By PROFESSOR ISLAY BURNS, D.D., Glasgow.

II.
Small crown 8vo, 3s. 6d. cloth, with Portrait.

MEMORIALS OF JAMES HENDERSON, M.D., F.R.C.S.E., Medical Missionary to China.

III.
16mo, 1s. cloth.

CHINA AND ITS PEOPLE. By a Missionary's Wife.

IV.
Small crown 8vo, 1s. sewed; 2s. cloth.

NARRATIVE OF THE MISSION TO CHINA OF THE PRESBYTERIAN CHURCH IN ENGLAND. By DONALD MATHESON, ESQ., formerly of China.

V.
Small crown 8vo, 2s. cloth.

MISSIONS TO THE WOMEN OF CHINA. Edited by MISS WHATELY.

VI.
Price 1½d., or 10s. 6d. per 100.

CHINA AND THE CHINESE MISSION. By the late JAMES HAMILTON, D.D.

HOME MISSIONS.

Small crown 8vo, 2s. cloth limp; 2s. 6d. cloth boards.

THEM ALSO. The Story of the Dublin Mission. By the Author of "Holly and Ivy," etc.

Small crown 8vo, 3s. 6d. cloth; 1s. 6d. cloth limp.

RAGGED HOMES, AND HOW TO MEND THEM. By MRS. BAYLEY.

Small crown 8vo, 3s. 6d. cloth boards; 1s. 6d cloth limp.

THE MISSING LINK; or, Bible Women in the Homes of the London Poor. By L. N. R.

Small crown 8vo, 2s. cloth.

LIFE WORK; or, the Link and the Rivet.

Small crown 8vo, 2s. cloth boards; 1s. limp cloth.

WORKMEN AND THEIR DIFFICULTIES. By MRS. BAYLEY.

Small crown 8vo, 3s. 6d. cloth; 1s. 6d. cloth limp.

HASTE TO THE RESCUE; or, Work while it is Day. By Mrs. CHARLES WIGHTMAN.

Small crown 8vo, 3s. 6d. cloth.

ANNALS OF THE RESCUED. By the Author of "Haste to the Rescue."

FOREIGN MISSIONS.

Small crown 8vo, 4s. 6d. cloth.

FAITH AND VICTORY; or, A Story of the Progress of Christianity in Bengal. By the late MRS. MULLENS.

Crown 8vo, 3s. 6d. cloth.

CIVILIZING MOUNTAIN MEN; or, Sketches of Mission Work among the Karens. By MRS. MASON, of Burmah.

8vo, 3s. 6d. cloth.

A BRIEF REVIEW OF TEN YEARS' MISSIONARY LABOUR in India between 1852 and 1863. Prepared from Local Reports and Original Letters. By the REV. DR. MULLENS.

8vo, 12s. cloth.

TEN YEARS IN SOUTH CENTRAL POLYNESIA; being Reminiscences of a Personal Mission to the Friendly Islands and their Dependencies. By the REV. THOMAS WEST.

LONDON: JAMES NISBET & CO., 21 BERNERS STREET.

www.ingramcontent.com/pod-product-compliance
Lightning Source LLC
Chambersburg PA
CBHW030808230426
43667CB00008B/1113